CARLITOS PRICE

BLOCKBUSTER FAITH

A 31-DAY DEVOTIONAL

CONTENTS

INTRODUCTION

What movie genre would you compare your life to? Perhaps a comedy filled with lots of embarrassing moments, like the first time I met my wife. Every Sunday morning, I would get up early and iron my clothes for service and neatly put them on the living room chair before going to take a shower. When I return to get dressed, I would watch a bit of TV before leaving for church. I recall one of those Sundays leaving my bedroom to go to the living room clad only in my boxers. As I grabbed my clothing, I heard a voice coming from behind me. "Good morning." No one had told me they were inviting anyone to our house, so I was confused for a moment. As I slowly turned, I came face to face with a beautiful young lady sitting on the chair. Now you can imagine how shameful that encounter was.

Maybe your life is filled with drama, lots of those highly emotional moments that seem unnecessary. Like, the time my wife (girlfriend at the time) walked into the living room of my parent's home and saw me and a friend in an intense argument. She said it had made her uncomfortable, more like downright furious, so she stormed out the door enraged. When I realized what had happened, I ran out the door in pursuit of the little ball of fury she was. An all-out verbal brawl ensued for the next couple of minutes in the middle of the road in front of what appeared to be the entire neighborhood.

Perhaps your life is an action adventure punctuated with new and exciting encounters. Or maybe it is a romance. Why is it that in romance movies the character must get to the airport to confess their love before the plane takes off? Can't they just call the next day? I hope your life isn't a horror filled with intense repugnance, fear, or dread. Perhaps you have a well-balanced mix of all the genres, which means your life will never have a dull moment.

Most of us like movies. We see ourselves in these characters as they strive to overcome obstacles and challenges, or we see in them what we wish we could be. I've seen myself as the knight in shining armor climbing up the balcony to rescue Vivian in *Pretty Woman*, and I have been King Leonidas leading the 300 into battle. I have also been Morpheus in The *Matrix Reloaded*, standing before the citizens of Zion.

I love movies and I love the Bible. There are moments when a scene, quote, or the plot, highlights a concept or principle from God's word, whether or not it was intended by the writers. The intention of this book isn't to encourage you to watch more TV, I am pretty sure that we are doing too much of that… I want to use some of the movies you are already familiar with to intrigue, illuminate, and inspire you to see the word of God, not just as something to be read, but to be lived. So, join me on this epic journey, one that will challenge and encourage you to be a disciple of Christ, one that requires blockbuster faith.

HE IS THE ONE

Movie: The Matrix (1999)

"When the Matrix was first built, there was a man born inside who had the ability to change whatever he wanted, to remake the Matrix as he saw fit. It was he who freed the first of us, taught us the truth. As long as the Matrix exists the human race will never be free. After he died, the Oracle prophesied his return and that his coming would hail the destruction of the Matrix, end the war, bring freedom to our people. That is why there are those of us who have spent our entire lives searching the Matrix looking for him. I did what I did because I believe that search is over." -Morpheus telling Neo of The One

Whenever a blockbuster movie is going to be released, there is a process that takes place. I call this building the hype. Events and press conferences are held, souvenirs and memorabilia are sold, and multiple trailers are released. The trailer gives the masses glimpses of what is to be expected in the movie. The hype about Jesus had been building for centuries from Genesis. Let us look at a couple of scriptures. **Genesis 3:15** *"And I will put enmity between you and the woman, and between your seed and her Seed; He shall bruise your head, and you shall bruise His heel."*

Isaiah 7: 14 *"Therefore the Lord Himself will give you a sign: Behold, the virgin shall conceive and bear a Son, and shall call His name Immanuel."*

The disciples must have started to put the pieces of the puzzle together. They grew up hearing about a person who would be sent by God to deliver them. One who would be like Moses who had led the Israelites out of Egyptian bondage. They were searching for this one Messiah who would restore the glory of the former Israelite kingdom. They must have heard about the child being born of a virgin. There must have been further confirmation when John baptized Him, and the heavens opened and the Spirit of God descended as a dove and a voice that I imagine to be thunderous said, *"this is my beloved son in whom I am well pleased."*

John 1:41 *"He first found his own brother Simon, and said to him, 'We have found the Messiah' (which is translated, the Christ)."* Andrew was a committed follower of John the Baptist, so when John pointed towards Jesus and declared that He was the lamb of God, Andrew quickly went to his brother to tell him he had found the One. When Jesus asked them to follow Him, I believe they had already made up in their minds that He was the One. Their search was over and they were going to follow Him wherever He led them.

In one of the final scenes in the Matrix, Neo is chased into a hallway and shot by Agent Smith until he slumps to the floor and dies. It is at this point that Trinity steps in and reveals that she was told she would fall in love with the one. This meant it was impossible for Neo to die at that moment because she loved him. Awwww. The heart monitor attached to Neo beeped and regained its rhythm. Neo gasped for breath and rises to face Agent Smith. In that moment, Morpheus' beliefs are fully realized, Neo was the one.

Of all the characters throughout history, only Jesus predicted and fulfilled his death. For some, this is difficult to believe as they doubt Jesus existed. And even if He did, they believe there is no evidence of Him being raised from the dead. I am convinced of this Jesus because of these men who saw Him and immediately knew He was the One they had been waiting for. There are historical records of these men being persecuted, tortured, and martyred, crucified upside down and right side up, and beheaded all in the name of this Jesus. When they met Him, they believed that their search was over. Jesus the Christ was the One.

There are so much YouTube videos with principles to follow to get the best out of life, however none of them can offer life itself. Jesus is the worthy figure to follow, and He is the One who can offer us life.

Reflection & Charge

I am not sure we spend enough time paying attention to His ideas and examples. Study the life and principles of Christ by reading through the four Gospels (Matthew, Mark, Luke, and John). Follow His journey from birth to resurrection and record the examples and perspective He left behind for us to follow.

DAY 2

THERE IS ONE I COULD FOLLOW

<u>Movie: The Hobbit: An Unexpected Journey (2012)</u>

In the Hobbit movie, the dwarves are in a battle against the orcs and it is not going in the dwarves' favor. The orc commander, Azog, has beheaded their king and they are on the brink of defeat. It is then Thorin the dwarf prince rises to take on the orc leader, and he is armed with nothing but an oak branch. He eventually grabs a sword from a fallen soldier and cuts off the hand of Azog, and this turns the tide of the battle in favor of the Dwarves. It is then Balin looks at Thorin in a new light and says, *"I thought to myself then, there is one I could follow. There is one I could call King."*

Matthew 4:18-20 *"And Jesus, walking by the Sea of Galilee, saw two brothers, Simon called Peter, and Andrew his brother, casting a net into the sea; for they were fishermen. Then He said to them, 'Follow Me, and I will make you fishers of men.' They immediately left their nets and followed Him."*

It is one thing to know He is the One, but you still have to decide to follow Him. The men in this scene left their nets and followed Jesus.

I have always wondered what would make a man leave his livelihood, his very source of income, his sense of manhood and follow Jesus in an instant. Was it the twinkle in His eye or the sound of His voice? Why did these men, or anyone, abandon their life and follow Jesus? In isolation, it might seem ridiculous for these men to just drop everything and follow Jesus, but upon further examination, we see from the reflection above that these men had been searching for Jesus possibly most of their lives.

We're all searching for something. I didn't realize it at the time, but I spent a portion of my youth searching for someone to emulate. Watching every episode of *The Fresh Prince* I thought I found my "hero". I yearned to be someone with an infectious personality. Later in life, I wanted to be a confident trendsetter, an artist with the most Grammy nominations, the first rapper to become a billionaire… I had all the CDs, wore the basketball jerseys, and fitted baseball caps. I even hung a giant poster on the wall to complete my altar to the rap superstar. Surely, he was worth following.

In our world today, people are searching for someone or something to follow. They are searching for answers to their questions…the truth about life. Our world is broken into two groups: influencers and followers. With the ease of access to information, I believe people are just searching for a way to navigate life. They spend their time looking for someone who can guide them through the chaos. Little do they know that there is a simple solution to their search. The person they are looking for, is the One who the disciples dropped everything for and followed.

Reflection & Charge:

We should evaluate the people we choose to follow carefully by asking ourselves some tough questions.

- Are they really worthy of our attention and devotion?
- Where are they going in life?
- Are you seeing the real them or just the person they want you to see?
- What are you searching for? Most importantly, who are you searching for?

Make a list of the people you currently follow on social media or otherwise, then compare them to the characteristics of Christ and decide if these people should remain as your source of leadership.

DAY 3

INSTITUTIONALIZED

Movie: Shawshank Redemption (1994)

"These walls are funny. First you hate 'em. Then you get used to 'em. Enough time passes, you get so you depend on them. That's institutionalized." -Red

In the Shawshank Redemption, Ellis is explaining why one of his fellow inmates, Brooks, attacked another inmate. Brooks had been incarcerated at a young age and spent most of his life behind the prison walls. He spent half a century as a citizen of Shawshank prison. When he was granted bail and given the opportunity to live as a free man, he was so afraid of leaving prison that he held one of his companions at knife point so that his prison stay would be extended. Can you picture fighting to stay in prison?

After being out in the real world, Brooks feels lonely and out of place. The world outside differs from what he remembered. Finding himself in the position of not being able to go back to prison, and not being able to navigate the unfamiliar world, he hangs himself.

When the people of Israel were released from captivity and oppression for over 400 years, they wandered in the desert between the prison of Egypt they had left behind and the land God promised them. Throughout their 40-year journey, they struggled to grasp the idea of being free. At the first sign of trouble, they would panic and be ready to go back to Egypt, the land of their oppression.

> **Exodus 14:10-12** *"And when Pharaoh drew near, the children of Israel lifted their eyes, and behold, the Egyptians marched after them. So they were very afraid, and the children of Israel cried out to the Lord. Then they said to Moses, 'Because there were no graves in Egypt, have you taken us away to die in the wilderness? Why have you so dealt with us, to bring us up out of Egypt? Is this not the word that we told you in Egypt, saying, Let us alone that we may serve the Egyptians?' For it would have been better for us to serve the Egyptians than that we should die in the wilderness."*

This scripture illustrates a picture that they were institutionalized. The Israelites would repeat this cycle throughout their journey. They were prisoners in Egypt for so long that they couldn't seem to leave it behind. In fact, most of those who left Egypt never saw or entered Canaan.

Does it seem as though your old life is chasing you down like Pharoah? Or maybe it is difficult to forget who you were before you received Christ. I have felt the pull myself to forget this new life in Christ and turn back to the life of what appears to be comfort and pleasure in sin, but is actually oppression and bondage. I have seen many people turn back from walking with the Lord. Some would argue that those people were never saved to begin with, but I am not so sure. The Israelites were physically free, but mentally still oppressed. Maybe people are spiritually free, but still mentally bound. They have known the sinful nature for so long that they have become institutionalized and there is a genuine struggle to walk with God. **Psalm 51:5** *"Behold, I was brought forth in iniquity, and in sin my mother conceived me."*

The walls of sin and our past lives can seem more comfortable than the life of a disciple. This is nothing but a tactic of the enemy. It is even harder when you are the only saved person in your home, at work, and among your peers. If a past cellmate was released with Brooks, perhaps he might have lived out his life naturally. Don't just be free spiritually, make it your business to be free from the mental bondages of your past.

Reflection & Charge

Is something from your past holding you prisoner even though Christ has freed you? **Yes/No.** If yes, what is it?

What steps are you going to take to walk in that freedom?

Empathize with those who are struggling and create an environment, a tribe, where they can have the freedom to be open about their struggles. List the different ways you believe you can offer your help. **Example:** spending quality time with them every month outside of a church setting.

DAY 4

MIND-BLOWN

Movie: Interstellar (2014)

Hebrews 11:3 *"By faith we understand that the worlds were framed by the word of God, so that the things which are seen were not made of things which are visible."*

There are some concepts that are harder to wrap our minds around than others. In the movie *Interstellar*, there is the idea of a black hole and time dilation. Time passes at different rates depending on your location. Time advances slower for those who are in the black hole than those who are back on earth. It is so extreme that one hour on the planet they are exploring is seven years on earth. In one scene, an astronaut leaves the ship for a few minutes and when he returns, the other astronaut had been waiting for two years. Although it is an exaggeration of a real phenomenon, it still blows my mind.

From the outset of the Bible, we are presented with a host of mind-blowing concepts. The first one is in Genesis 1:2. The author depicts the setting as one of emptiness; he uses the terms formless and void. This meant there was nothing: no land or sea, birds or fish, no structures were in place, it was just space.

It goes onto say in verse 3, *"then God said, 'Let there be light'; and there was light."* Creative symphony orchestrated by the words of the Creator. I once encountered a student in Sunday School who asked, *"If God created everything who created God?"* There was only one response to that question: *"God was not created, He always existed."* Mind-blowing, isn't it?

There are many other mind-blowing concepts in the Old Testament: the floods that covered the earth, oceans that split apart, men who walked out of a fire and came out unscathed. But I want to go to the New Testament for a minute and talk about Jesus. There was no earthly male DNA, but Jesus was conceived through the Holy Spirit in the womb of the Virgin Mary. Jesus Christ, the Messiah, was not just man, but also God. Isn't that also mind-blowing? Thirty-three years later, this same Jesus was arrested, tortured, and put to death by crucifixion. His body was laid to rest in a tomb. But three days later, He rose from the dead. Once again, another mind-blowing event.

Most people cannot wrap their minds around a God that had no beginning. Or a Jesus who is God and man, or a human being raised from the dead after three days. I am certain God doesn't expect us to understand or explain it. Nonetheless, He does require us to accept by faith.

Here is my belief, everything that has a beginning has an end. God had no beginning; therefore, He has no end. He was, is, and always will be. To some, Jesus being God and man when He walked the earth doesn't fully compute. But the good news is, since God has no end, it only makes sense that Jesus would also have no end. This was solidified when Jesus was crucified, but rose from the dead and is still alive today. Our faith in Him gives us the privilege of eternal life after our bodies perish. Mind-blowing.

Hebrews 11:6 *"But without faith it is impossible to please Him, for he who comes to God must believe that He is, and that He is a rewarder of those who diligently seek Him."*

As a believer in Christ, there are some aspects of God that will always remain a mystery. Some things about Him are just indescribable. One of those aspects is that He exists outside of time. My view of life is limited to the years I spend on this earth, while God's view is the entirety of history and the future all at once. I compare it to one of those elaborate domino chain reactions that people do for fun. My life is just one domino amid an innumerable number of other lives. While I can only comprehend my domino, God sees the entire chain reaction. This means I must go against my natural inclination to understand every aspect of the process. It means I have to entrust my life to Him, even though I will not understand everything.

I challenge you to think differently about the time you will spend on this earth. It is a mere wrinkle in the fabric of eternity, so think of it as an investment of what is to come. Make a declaration to God and yourself that you will trust Him by obeying His commands, even those that are seemingly difficult to understand.

Reflection & Charge

Make a list of the things that seem mind-blowing to you. Lay them before God and ask Him for clarity. For the things you don't receive an answer for, make a bold declaration that you will trust Him regardless of the things you don't understand.

DAY 5

THE PLOT TWIST

Movie: Star Wars: Episode 5 "The Empire Strikes Back (1980)

Darth Vader: *"If you only knew the power of the Dark Side. Obi-Wan never told you what happened to your father."*

Luke: *"He told me enough! He told me *you* killed him!"*

Darth Vader: *"No. *I* am your father."*

A plot twist is that revelation in your favorite story that blows your mind or changes the course of the viewing experience. One of the most memorable and iconic plot twists in film history is when Darth Vader reveals his true identity to Luke. I have discovered that we also experience plot twists, life-changing events that change or interrupt, maybe even derail the planned trajectory of our lives. This may be the birth of a child, the discovery of an illness, loss of a job, death of a loved one.

There is a plot twist I believe we all must experience and even embrace to live the life that God intends for us. Hold on to your socks. I know in the story of your life you are the main character; and you view yourself as the hero. But it is important to understand that you are not the hero. I would even take it further and say that this is not really your story. Just think about your life, you had no say on where or when you were born, the color of your skin, your physical appearance, or your talents.

Just ask Mr. Roundtree if you don't believe me. Think Old School Dub, 1995. A line in his song goes, "I wish I was a little bit…" You honestly have to admit that you have little control when it comes to your life. God, the Creator and originator of all life, is the One who authors the story of our existence, and we get minor roles or subplots in His grand blockbuster event.

Do you know you are actually a villain? Romans 3:23 says, *"for all have sinned and fall short of the glory of God."* Our condition of sin makes us enemies of God. Another dimension to this revelation of us being on the dark side of the story is that we have all played the villain in someone else's life. We have been the one to say something that turned someone's day or life upside down. We have been the inconsiderate family member, the person who said something hurtful, etc. No matter how good we think we have been, we have all fallen short, we have all played the villain.

Jesus said these words in response to someone calling Him good. **Mark 10:18** *"So Jesus said to him, 'Why do you call Me good? No one is good but One, that is, God.'"* If Jesus said no one is good, then what hope is there for the rest of us? This is not an attempt to make you feel sorry for yourself or to bring you down. Well, maybe we all need a healthy dose of reality about who we are. Perhaps the idea of our villainous nature will help us remember who we are when we look down on those who seem not to be as good as we are. When we think we are perfect, we exhibit self-righteous behavior like the man in the scripture below.

Luke 18:11-12 *"The Pharisee stood and prayed thus with himself, 'God, I thank You that I am not like other men—extortioners, unjust, adulterers, or even as this tax collector. I fast twice a week; I give tithes of all that I possess.'"*

Reflection & Charge

Remember I said, this is not about pulling you down, but helping you see we can be a villain intentionally or unintentionally. How do you feel about being lumped with the likes of Darth Vader, the Terminator, or even the Joker?

When was the last time you were the villain in someone's story?

When did you last experience a villain?

Have you forgiven them as yet?

If no, what is stopping you from doing so?

WHO COULD LOVE A BEAST?

Movie: Beauty and the Beast: Animated (1991)

"As the years passed, he fell into despair and lost all hope. For who could ever learn to love a beast?" -Beauty and the Beast

A couple of days before I preached a sermon, I asked the members of the congregation a question to increase the level of engagement. "What do you think is my favorite movie genre?" I then gave some options for them to choose from. They were action/adventure, science-fiction/fantasy, horror, romance, and comedy. The congregation strongly leaned towards sci-fi/fantasy. Even though I love that genre, my favorite is romance. It is one that I guard carefully and keep to myself. Why? As you could guess, it is not very appealing for men to admit this genre as their favorite.

Who wants to admit to a group of guys that one of your favorite scenes in *Pretty Woman* is when Edward climbs up the ladder to become Vivian's knight in shining armor? Or that scene from *Love & Basketball* when after playing one on one for his heart, Monica turns to walk away in defeat, but Quincy stops her by saying, "double or nothing." Yea, you won't find me admitting that under "normal" circumstances. But here I am.

The theme of love is woven throughout all genres. Aragon and Arwen in *The Lord of the Rings*, Neo and Trinity in *The Matrix*, Princess Leia and Han Solo in *Star Wars*. We really can't escape the element of love, or at least what love is portrayed to be on the screen.

Love is also embedded in the stories of the Bible. In fact, God is synonymous with love. **1 John 4:7-8** *"Beloved, let us love one another, for love is of God; and everyone who loves is born of God and knows God. He who does not love does not know God, for God is love."* Love is mostly associated with flowers, teddy bears, slow music, dimmed lights, rose petals, and calming aromas. Society believes falling in love is sweaty palms, butterflies in the stomach, and long conversations on the telephone. The problem with this philosophy is that in most cases these feelings don't last and falling out of love comes next. The Bible paints the picture of something more rugged. The visual I get for love is that of nail-pierced hands, and blood and water flowing from the side of Jesus as He is crucified on behalf of humanity.

In *Beauty and the Beast*, Belle, a beautiful, kind-hearted daughter, offers to take the place of her beloved father as the prisoner of an ugly, selfish, and unkind Beast with no love in his heart. During her stay with the Beast, she eventually cares for him, and they fall in love. In the end, they broke the curse and lived happily ever after.

Who are the characters we root for in stories? The kind, beautiful ones with pure hearts, or the ugly and coldhearted villains? From my observation, we want the former ones to live, while we welcome the defeat or destruction of the latter ones who we deem as undeserving. The picture of love from Jesus Christ is very different. In this story we are the Beast, the undeserving who cares for no one else but ourselves, while Christ in His pure state was willing to demonstrate His love for us by dying on the cross. **Romans 5:8** *"But God demonstrates His own love toward us, in that while we were still sinners, Christ died for us."*

This really illustrates the idea of love as less of a feeling and emotion, to one of choice. We have to see the value in every human despite the degree to which we believe they deserve it. When we do that, we can then answer the question, "who could ever learn to love a Beast?" Because we would know that Jesus Christ did. We cannot treat people based on how they make us feel, Jesus commands us to love unconditionally. It means it is not an option; it is quite mandatory. Love is the trait that identifies us as disciples, and it is our actions toward one another despite our feelings that show the love that God gave us even in our ugly and sinful state.

Reflection & Charge

God can love a "Beast" even if you don't always feel like they are lovable or deserving of love. Choose small acts of kindness to people you encounter who may not always behave kind. Be determined every day to act in love despite the attitudes and behaviors of others.

When you think about love, what image comes to mind?

Do you believe love can be truly unconditional? If so, why?

Do you think of yourself as worthy of love despite your mistakes?

Do you think that the "Beasts" in your life are worthy of love?

What will you do differently to show the unconditional love of God?

DAY 7

WHO AM I?

<u>Movie: The Bourne Identity (2002)</u>

The scene opens with the silhouette of a lifeless body floating in water during a stormy night. A group of fishermen discover the body and pull it aboard their fishing boat. One of the fishermen, Giancarlo, takes the responsibility of looking after the stranger. He removes two bullets from the back of the unconscious man and a small device embedded in his hip with the name of a bank and an account number. When the stranger suddenly awakens, he is confused about what happened to him and where he is. Giancarlo introduces himself in an attempt to calm his newfound companion and then asks for his name, to which he responds, *"I don't know."* In the rest of the movie, the stranger from the water, Jason Bourne, sets on a quest to discover who he really is.

Jason Bourne, like many of us, struggles to discover his identity. His special skills and abilities give him clues to his origins, but he still does not truly unearth who he is until he returns to where everything began. How would you answer the question *who am I?* Maybe you will say, "I am a father, a Christian, a male." I am sure you could produce a list of descriptions, talents, and characteristics about yourself, but to truly discover who you are, you must return to the source.

Your identity is complex and can be stolen. We can be confused about who we are, which is an **identity crisis**. We can even assume the persona of someone else, which is **mistaken identity**. One aspect of identity which we must all grapple with and eventually accept is that we don't get to choose who we are. We are who we are by God's design.

Matthew 4:1-3 *"Then Jesus was led up by the Spirit into the wilderness to be tempted by the devil. And when He had fasted forty days and forty nights, afterward He was hungry. Now when the tempter came to Him, he said, 'If You are the Son of God, command that these stones become bread.'"*

Before Jesus preaches about the Kingdom of Heaven, the Devil tempts him. This trial by fire moment was a necessary part of Jesus' journey while He was on earth. He was led into temptation by the Spirit of God. The passage continues by saying that after 40 days without food or water, He was hungry, evidence of the dual nature of Jesus. Though He was God, He was also a man who felt hunger and faced all the frailties that come with humanity.

Jesus' heritage in Matthew 1 can be traced back to that of Abraham, Isaac, Jacob, Ruth, Boaz, King David, and Solomon, which solidified that He was man. However, after Jesus is baptized by John the Baptist, the gates of Heaven open and the clouds part. The Spirit of God takes the form of a dove and descends upon Jesus. This event affirmed the Sonship/identity of Christ as the Son of God. Satan begins the conflict by bringing to question the very thing that had just been affirmed by God Himself. Everything that Satan offered Jesus was already His, and Jesus did not fall into temptation because He knew who He was.

- **"If You are the Son of God, command that these stones become bread."**

  "But He answered and said, 'It is written, Man shall not live by bread alone, but by every word that proceeds from the mouth of God.'" Matthew 4:4

- **"If You are the Son of God, throw Yourself down."**

  "Jesus said to him, 'It is written again, You shall not tempt the Lord your God.'" Matthew 4:7

- **"All these things I will give You if You will fall down and worship me."**

  "Away with you, Satan! For it is written, 'You shall worship the Lord your God, and Him only you shall serve.'" Matthew 4:10

We never have to live up to the expectations and standards of any human or entity other than God Himself. Satan can use this tactic on us by challenging our Christian experience. *"If you are a child of God, then why haven't you received an answer to that prayer? Why are you still struggling with this issue?"*

We must know who we are and its implications. There are things that Satan will offer us out of the context that God has designed. It can be dangerous for us to receive a blessing before the God appointed time. The right thing obtained in the wrong way is still the wrong thing. The right thing obtained at the wrong time is still the wrong thing. So, who are you? You were created in the image of God with great capacity for creativity, compassion, empathy, mercy, and love.

Reflection & Charge

Like Jason Bourne, I believe you must return to your Creator to find your identity. Spend some time searching the Bible and discover your true identity in Christ. Here are a few to get you started.

Romans 8:17 "Heirs of God"

Matthew 5:13-14 "Salt & Light"

Romans 8:37 "Conquerors"

THE HUNGER GAMES

Movie: The Hunger Games (2012)

The fictional country Panem comprises of the Capitol and thirteen districts. Each year, representatives are selected against their will to compete in the hunger games. These games are a competition of skill and survival. The competitors use bows, knives, poisons, spears; absolutely anything they can to make sure they win because the contest is one to death. Katniss Everdeen, the tribute who volunteered to enter the hunger games in place of her sister, is defiant throughout the four movies. She helps to redirect the attention of the hunger games. Instead of the districts fighting against and killing each other, she encouraged them to be part of the resistance, fighting against the real enemy, the Capitol.

Our present-day Christianity feels like spiritual hunger games. Different denominations, churches and Christian groups are in a battle royale. The thinking seems to be that only one can be right, so every other group must be destroyed. Well, maybe not destroyed, but at least proven wrong. There are a lot of YouTube channels dedicated to pointing out the errors in the doctrine of preachers and leaders.

What I see in the Christian community both saddens and scares me. I constantly find myself watching videos to make sure what I am teaching is accurate and doesn't go against what that Christian teacher has pointed out as being wrong. This of course is a futile endeavor since each person seems to find fault with everything.

One sure way of creating unity among parties is to identify a common enemy. There is a desperate need to refocus our efforts on fighting spiritual forces instead of physical ones. My belief is that our focus should be turned towards the real enemy and his principles and strategies.

Ephesians 6:10-13 *"Finally, my brethren, be strong in the Lord and in the power of His might. Put on the whole armor of God, that you may be able to stand against the wiles of the devil. For we do not wrestle against flesh and blood, but against principalities, against powers, against the rulers of the darkness of this age, against spiritual hosts of wickedness in the heavenly places. Therefore take up the whole armor of God, that you may be able to withstand in the evil day, and having done all, to stand."*

The scripture clearly says that they are forces in the spiritual realm we must be aware of and be prepared to face. It further states that we are not fighting against other humans; we must refocus our efforts towards the false principles and ideas of our spiritual enemy. We need to remember that the other Christian denominations/groups are on our side and the real enemy is Satan.

In the parable of the wheat and the tares in Matthew 13:24-30, a farmer sows seeds of wheat. After a period of time, an enemy sows tares in the field and the tares and the wheat grow together, making it difficult to differentiate between the two. When the workers ask the landowner if they should attempt to pull up the wheat, he responds by telling them that this exercise could cause the wheat to be harmed.

We are doing more damage than good when we attack each other. All it does is create uncertainty and insecurity in the hearts of those who are trying to follow Christ. I do believe there are some very dangerous and inaccurate principles being taught. However, that is not the case with everyone we are fighting. Just because we differ in opinions does not mean we have to destroy each other.

Yes, there are some people who are preaching for their own gain. Paul addresses this in **Philippians 1:15-18** *"Some indeed preach Christ even from envy and strife, and some also from goodwill: The former preach Christ from selfish ambition, not sincerely, supposing to add affliction to my chains; but the latter out of love, knowing that I am appointed for the defense of the gospel. What then? Only that in every way, whether in pretense or in truth, Christ is preached; and in this I rejoice, yes, and will rejoice."*

I honestly believe that most preachers are doing so genuinely, without trying to rob or manipulate the saints. With that view in mind, we should dedicate ourselves to pray for those we think are on the wrong track. And for ourselves in case we too have also had our intentions twisted along the way. There are many points that we can find in our doctrinal beliefs that don't align with another person's. But why not follow the idea that Paul wrote about in Romans 14:19 and do whatever we can to live in peace with each other? There are other Christians who won't hold to every idea you have, but how about finding things that you have in common? Always remember you are fighting the same enemy, and maybe it will help you stop fighting each other.

Reflection & Charge

How do you feel about Christians from other denominations?

Why do you feel the way you do? Is it because of something you were told?

How do you contribute to the disunity that exists within the body of Christ?

What can you do to close the gap that exists between different denominations?

What can the church do to close the gap that exists between different denominations?

ANOTHER SEASON IS COMING!

Movie: Batman v Superman: Dawn of Justice (2016)

I have always been a big Superman fan; I mean how could anyone not be? He is faster than a speeding bullet, more powerful than a locomotive, and able to leap tall buildings in a single bound. I even once tried to convince my mother to change my name to Superman, but obviously she didn't go for it. In the Batman v Superman movie. There is a battle between Superman and Doomsday, a story that has also been told in an animated movie and the comics.

This is one of the toughest battles Superman has ever faced, he and the seemingly indestructible foe Doomsday wreck the city in an all-out brawl. In the end, Superman is victorious. However, he succumbs to the beating he received during the fight and dies. Yes, he dies, or at least it appears that way. But how can he be dead? Isn't he the hero? Isn't he supposed to continue to save the day? Clearly, this couldn't be the end of the story, there had to be more…more time in the movie or maybe a sequel.

One thing that has never sat well with me, and I believe most of us, is the idea that we must die. We are born; we go through infancy, puberty; go to school, overcome bullies, get jobs, fall in love, endure heartbreaks, encounter sickness, disappointments, some of us have kids, we write books, sing songs, and win medals. All of this and then we just die.

Death can be extremely difficult. When we lose someone who is close to us, we find it hard to accept. I used to have dreams that felt real about my uncle years after he had passed away. We would have conversations about the Matrix sequels or the Lord of the Rings movies, neither of which he was alive to see, but I know he would have been a great fan.

According to the Bible, I can safely say that we were never meant to die. The penalty of death was introduced because of the disobedience of the first two humans. That sin factor just ruined everything. I have hypothesized therefore that a sliver of eternity has been sown somewhere within us. This longing to live forever has challenged man to try to find the fountain of youth, literally and figuratively. It is as if we know somehow that we were not meant to die.

Romans 6:23 *"For the wages of sin is death, but the gift of God is eternal life in Christ Jesus our Lord.* I am not trying to add doom and gloom, but I want to paint the entire picture. We have all sinned and fallen short of the glory of God. So, death is inevitable for all of us. The movie *Final Destination* paints an over dramatized picture of the reality of not being able to escape death, at least naturally.

If you have a Netflix account, you know that they have become prolific in releasing their own original movies and series. Some of these series are extremely popular, so when they end, Netflix does not let their viewers suffer with expectation of the continuance of that show. Once they decide to renew the show, they have a notice on the show's menu. It reads, *"It's official: another season is coming."* The viewers stop holding their breath, knowing that the story will not end soon.

Well, I want to ease your anxiety about your story. If you have received Jesus Christ as your Lord and Savior, then death is not the end of life, but merely a pause between seasons. It is official, another season is coming. Your life will continue in eternity with Christ in Heaven.

1 Corinthians 15:51-53 *"Behold, I tell you a mystery: We shall not all sleep, but we shall all be changed— in a moment, in the twinkling of an eye, at the last trumpet. For the trumpet will sound, and the dead will be raised incorruptible, and we shall be changed. For this corruptible must put on incorruption, and this mortal must put on immortality."*

Reflection & Charge

I truly believe that the bonds we create were meant to last forever and not be interrupted by death. This life on earth must be followed by something more. The good news of Jesus Christ's victory over death is too great an accomplishment to keep to ourselves.

Write the names of two people below and share the great news with them this week.

Do you accept that there is more than just the life you live on this earth?

How does the idea of an afterlife affect the way you live your life today?

FREE YOUR MIND

Movie: The Matrix (1999)

"You have to let it all go Neo - fear, doubt, disbelief. Free your mind." -Morpheus

As human beings, we will come face to face with "our" limitations at some point. We all come to that inevitable border separating the possible from the impossible. When Neo is introduced to the jump program as part of his training, he struggles to accept that his limitations no longer exist. He watches as Morpheus makes an impossible jump from the top of one building to the other with little effort.

When it is his turn, he examines the drop from the top of the building and then turns to walk as far back as he could to get the longest run up possible. This was an indicator that he was still thinking in terms of a physical effort to accomplish the task, instead of the mental leap he needed to defy gravity. He runs, and like every other person before, he cannot make it and falls to a painful halt at the foot of the building.

In Mark 9:14-29, Jesus encounters a child with an evil spirit which His disciples could not cast out after many attempts. The child's father begs Jesus to intervene. Verses 22-24 *"'…But if You can do anything, have compassion on us and help us.' Jesus said to him, 'If you can believe, all things are possible to him who believes.' Immediately the father of the child cried out and said with tears, 'Lord, I believe; help my unbelief!'"*

The father, like Neo, struggles with unbelief and doubt. His asking was more of a last-ditch effort than a complete investment of faith. The statement, *"All things are possible to him who believes,"* makes me ask questions. Is the impossible just a function of our unbelief? Does this verse apply now as it did then? Does it mean that whatever we want we can have if we have enough faith?

I will not pretend that I know how to answer these questions definitively, but I know that this statement inspires me to see the world differently. I can boldly say that what is impossible with man is possible with God. The entire narrative of the Bible is based on the idea of this invisible being who can do anything. Over and over, we see Him defy the laws of science and nature to accomplish His purpose. How then can I not live a life believing that whatever He has called me to, He has the power to accomplish? No matter how impossible it may seem, I am confident that He can get it done.

There is a constant need for us to free our minds, and this can be accomplished by looking at the scriptures. We must recognize that the God we read about is not a fictional character and allow our minds to be freed by the truth in the Bible. At some point, you will face a problem that is beyond your power, knowledge, or resources to solve. I can't promise that if you believe hard enough it will change, and you will live happily ever after. However, I want to challenge you to believe that God can and will do whatever is best. The solution to your problem might very well be to leave things as they are.

I remember being with my classmates at a picnic when I was 11 years old. We stood at the edge of a cliff, which seemed steep at the time, and there was great debate among us on whether it was something we could safely do. In the midst of this intense discussion, I took the leap because I believed I would land safely in the sand below. This was faith in action despite the debate. I let go, and thankfully it ended well.

When Jesus was in Gethsemane praying before His crucifixion, there seemed to be a great debate within Him. He asked the Father to spare Him from having to drink from the cup; nonetheless, He surrendered to the will of God and submitted Himself to the soldiers. This was obedience and faith even in the face of death.

The three Hebrew boys were told to bow down to an idol or be thrown into a furnace, but they stayed true to their faith in God. If we are thrown into a blazing furnace, the God we serve is able to deliver us from it. They knew He could do the impossible, but they were also determined to stay true to Him even if He didn't come to their rescue. Let go of the fear and doubt, disbelief, and free your mind. Whatever God does is well done, and it will bring about a beautiful end. Ask God for the courage to take the leap even with the fears and doubts. As long as you believe God has called you to take action, take the leap.

Reflection & Charge

Do you have any fears that are holding you back from obeying God?

Where did those fears come from? Was it past rejection or something else?

What are some things you will do if you knew you could not fail?

Search the scripture for people who took the leap despite the uncertainty and show their outcome. Use this as an encouragement when doubt tries to sabotage you.

CHRISTENDOM FOREVER

Movie: Black Panther (2018)

Nestled somewhere in East Africa lies the fictional country of Wakanda. To outsiders it is a third world country inhabited by farmers and shepherds. However, the true nature of Wakanda is one that has been hidden for centuries. It is one of the most technologically advanced societies on earth and is rich in the otherworldly element: vibranium. Vibranium is an almost indestructible metal used in many of their tools and equipment, including their weapons.

Wakanda is ruled by a king who usually adopts the role of the Black Panther, the protector of the people. The King of Wakanda (T'Challa) realizes that while they were protecting themselves from outsiders, people all over the world could have benefited from their resources and technology.

Jesus taught the disciples to pray in Matthew 6. In verse 10, He instructs them to ask their Heavenly Father to allow His Kingdom to come, and His will be done on earth as it is in heaven. In other words, He was telling them to ask for the attributes of Heaven to be emulated on Earth. Imagine having Earth resemble Heaven where there is peace, harmony, no lack, or sickness.

When Jesus walked the earth, He repeatedly said to repent, for the Kingdom of Heaven is at hand. Wherever He went, He did good. He taught the principles of Heaven; He healed those who were sick; He released people from oppressive evil spirits and changed the lives of many. It is my belief that once we join the ranks of Christendom, we become ambassadors for the Kingdom of God. No matter where we are on Earth, we form a heavenly diaspora with a connection to spiritual resources unavailable to those who are not citizens.

When Daniel and the other Hebrews were taken captive by the Babylonians, he was placed among the brightest and the best. Daniel excelled among this group because of his relationship with God. The king had a mysterious dream and none of his advisors could tell him the meaning, so he promises to kill all the advisors unless an interpretation was revealed. Daniel recognized that his life and the lives of his colleagues were in danger, so he files a petition with his King (God) to intervene in the situation. Jehovah sends a swift reply, and Daniel's request is granted. He had the solution to a problem that no one could find.

There are many problems in our world that seemingly have no solution: people with mental health issues, identity crisis, dysfunctional relationships, economic struggles, these are just to name a few. How can we who are connected to this heavenly kingdom see these dark challenges and not access the spiritual resources at our disposal? Are we called to solve every problem, maybe not, but we are to use our connection to the unlimited resources of Heaven to shine light in the darkness.

I believe the reason we don't have more impact on our communities is because we are not truly convinced of what we have. In Acts 3, Peter and John encountered a lame man who begged them for money, their response to his plea was this, *"Silver and gold I do not have, but what I do have I give you: In the name of Jesus Christ of Nazareth, rise up and walk."* They were so convinced of Jesus' power to heal that they offered it to this man, and he was healed.

I am not suggesting that you are supposed to heal every lame or blind person, but there is no limit to what God can accomplish; the possibilities are endless. There are needs that can be fulfilled with what we have, we just have to meet them head on with whatever God has given us.

Reflection and Charge

Do you believe in all that God has given you? The power to heal and deliver? **Yes/No**. If no, what is stopping you from believing?

Search the Bible for scriptures that speak to who you are and what you have, and constantly rehearse those scriptures until they reside in your heart.

Make a list of problems you see in our society.

Ask God to show what steps you should take in order to bring a solution to these problems and write them below.

DAY 12

REMEMBER THE NAME

<u>Movie: Troy (2004)</u>

Triopas: *"Who are you, soldier?"*

Achilles: *"Achilles, son of Peleus."*

Triopas: *"Achilles? I'll remember the name."*

A champion is a person who has defeated or surpassed all rivals in a competition, especially in sports. We love and adore them; we follow their posts and hang on their every word; we watch and cheer as they assert their dominance in whatever field they play. Ali, Michael, Usain…their names are etched in our minds and hearts forever.

In the story of Troy, the kings of two opposing armies decide to engage in the battle strategy of single combat. This is where a champion is chosen from each side to represent the entire battle. Boagrius, the champion from the army of Thessaly, faces Achilles of the Greeks. It only takes seconds, and Achilles brings his opponent to his knees. His victory meant that the Greeks were victorious and soldiers from both sides did not need to fight.

In that moment, Achilles represented every Greek soldier. Their hope rested on him. I think this is what we like about champions; as we watch them in their respective arenas on the court, field, or track, they carry all of our hope of victory. Their win is our win. It is more than a race; it is the victory over all the hurdles and opponents in our lives, and for that we remember their names.

We see this occur in the Bible when the Israelite army stands against the Philistine army. A champion from Gath (Goliath) taunts the Israelites. **1 Samuel 17:8-9** *"Then he stood and cried out to the armies of Israel, and said to them, 'Why have you come out to line up for battle? Am I not a Philistine, and you the servants of Saul? Choose a man for yourselves, and let him come down to me. If he is able to fight with me and kill me, then we will be your servants. But if I prevail against him and kill him, then you shall be our servants and serve us.'"*

Only David, an inexperienced warrior and shepherd, is brave, or naïve enough to step out against this Philistine who defied the army of God. He was willing to face him in a single combat. It doesn't take long for David to defeat his foe and bring victory to the Israelites. David is hailed a champion and the people of Israel chant his name, *"Saul has killed his thousands, but David tens of thousands."*

There is one foe that even the greatest of us cannot overcome. Death has reigned as the undefeated champion since the time of Adam. Like taxes, death is the one thing that cannot be negotiated, it is certain. However, Jesus entered the arena with death and defeated it. Philippians says that Jesus became obedient to death, even death on the cross.

It would have appeared to those around Him that Jesus had been defeated by death. For three days, death seemed to hold Jesus captive, but after day three, those who searched for His body found an empty tomb. Jesus was alive and death had been defeated, a new champion had been crowned and the world would never forget His name. All those who put their faith in Christ now stand behind Him, the champion who conquered death made a way for us. **Philippians 2:9** *"Therefore God also has highly exalted Him and given Him the name which is above every name."*

If we are being honest, some names carry more weight than others. In my workplace, things get done immediately and expeditiously if the name of a certain director is mentioned. There are names that can get us into doors that would otherwise be closed. Ultimately, there is only one name that we should rest all our hope on. It is your duty to remember the name of the champion who stared death in the face and won on your behalf: Jesus Christ. **Acts 4:12** *"Nor is there salvation in any other, for there is no other name under heaven given among men by which we must be saved."*

Reflection & Charge

Take a survey of your life, whose name do you truly rely on?

Whose name are you trying to build up and promote? Yours or someone else's?

Think of ways you can contribute to promoting the name of Jesus Christ.

OATHBREAKERS

Movie: Lord of the Rings: The Return of the King (2003)

Elrond: *"You're outnumbered, Aragorn. You need more men."*

Aragorn: *"There are none."*

Elrond: *"There are those who dwell in the mountain."*

Aragorn: *"Murderers. Traitors. You would call upon them to fight? They believe in nothing. They answer to no one."*

Elrond: *"They will answer to the king of Gondor."*

In Lord of the Rings: Return of the King, Aragorn, the heir to the throne of Gondor, commands an army of ghosts and leads them into battle. Centuries earlier, this army of the dead were once known as the Men of the Mountains. They had made an oath to Isildur, the King of Gondor to come and aid him in the fight against the dark Lord Sauron. When the time came for them to join the battle, they ran and hid in the mountains, breaking their oath. Isildur cursed these Oathbreakers to live without rest until they fulfill their oath.

To be labeled an Oathbreaker is a heavy burden. The reality that you have not lived up to a promise that you have made, to know that you are in fact a traitor to some degree is a heart wrenching feeling. My college roommate and I did everything together. We played basketball, had versus battles, and even dressed alike. We were a regular dynamic duo. It wasn't long before a creature of the fairer sex crossed my path and like a lovesick puppy, I turned all of my attention to her, abandoning my roommate. I later discovered that while I was in my love trance, that roommate went through a tough time in his life and could have really used the support, but I was missing from the field of battle. I was an Oathbreaker.

Whether you realize or not, those who call themselves believers in Christ have made oaths as well. To be a Christian is to be His follower and therefore we sign up to His mission and purpose. Jesus calls Himself the light of the world and then extends that same moniker to us. We are mandated to let our light shine so men may see us and glorify God in heaven. I sometimes think of the Church and the thought that comes to mind is: Oathbreakers.

I sometimes feel as though we are absent from the impending darkness that exists in our world. Our presence in our schools and communities is almost non-existent. Like Peter, we boldly proclaim that we would stand by Christ, but when the time comes, we deny Him not wanting to be offensive or ridiculed by the masses. In the account of the crucifixion, have you noticed the lack of presence by the disciples? That is because they all fled in fright and hid. **Matthew 26:56** *"But all this was done that the Scriptures of the prophets might be fulfilled. Then all the disciples forsook Him and fled."*

Aragorn, the heir of Isildur, the only one who could release the Men of the Mountains from their curse, ventures into the mountains and enlists them to fight for him. He offers them a second chance to fulfil their oaths, to move from Oathbreakers to promise keepers. Peter and the disciples also received their redemption and some of them died horrible deaths, fulfilling those oaths to Jesus Christ.

I want to be known for the faithfulness to the promises I make; I want people to say I was a man of my word. As a believer, I want to be a promise keeper. I want to show up for the battle, even though it may be difficult to navigate the nuances of this world with groups and individuals who have agendas that oppose my belief system. Even though I will be labeled negatively, I want to be in the fight. I am willing to endure the persecution that comes from following Christ so that others might see who He is.

Reflection & Charge

One of the biggest promises you must keep as a believer is to show up for Him, to let others know you are with Christ even when it is not popular or politically correct. Think of ways you can keep your promise to represent Jesus in your everyday life.

What promises have you broken?

How can you make good on the promises you have made to others?

Have you ever said, "God if you help me I will
_______________________________________." *Fill in the blank.*

Have you lived up to that promise? If no, then why not?

DAY 14

THE GREAT EQUALIZER

Movie: The Equalizer (2014)

If there is one thing I believe garners no disagreement from any person, is that life is unfair. The disparity in our world is vast and repulsive. The world's richest 1% have more than twice the wealth of 6.9 million people, while half the population live on less than $5.50 a day. Men own 50% more wealth than women. There are some places in the world where children are denied education (258 million), and in some countries girls are not allowed to attend school.

Some of us will work hard all our lives, 8 hours a day, 5 days a week, and never amass the wealth of an 18-year-old who can throw a ball through a hoop. Some of us are born with no health problems, while others suffer their whole lives with physical and mental ailments from which they never recover. Life is definitely unfair.

Robert McCall is a man with unique skills which allow him to take on any foe. He uses these skills to defend the helpless and the weak. I see Jesus as the great equalizer. He takes people from all backgrounds and places them on the same level. While we might separate ourselves in classes, Jesus ignores the class lines and boundaries to show His unconditional love to all.

In John 4, Jesus is sitting at a well in Samaria when a woman comes to draw water. We are never told her name, but she is known by most Christians as the Samaritan woman. Their exchange is significant for multiple reasons: 1. She was Samaritan. 2. Jesus was a Jew. These two groups were never associated with each other. The other thing is that as a Rabbi, he should not talk directly to a woman. This is clear by the surprise of the disciples when they return and saw Jesus talking with her.

John 4:27 *"And at this point His disciples came, and they marveled that He talked with a woman; yet no one said, 'What do You seek?' or, 'Why are You talking with her?'"* This encounter with Jesus marked a turning point in the life of this woman, but it also showed the way Jesus saw women. This woman took the message of Jesus Christ to the men in town, forever placing her as one of the great evangelists of the Bible.

Another example of Jesus' role as equalizer is in the story of Lazarus and the rich man. The rich man enjoyed life because of the wealth he had, while Lazarus longed to eat the crumbs from the rich man's table. They both died (death is another equalizer). The rich man ends up tormented in hell while Lazarus goes to Heaven to live in comfort. **Luke 16:25** *"But Abraham said, 'Son, remember that in your lifetime you received your good things, and likewise Lazarus evil things; but now he is comforted and you are tormented.'"* What does the story illustrate? It conveys that your background does not determine where you will spend eternity. With all his riches, the rich man could not buy his way into Heaven.

Galatians 3:26-29 *"For you are all sons of God through faith in Christ Jesus. For as many of you as were baptized into Christ have put on Christ. There is neither Jew nor Greek, there is neither slave nor free, there is neither male nor female; for you are all one in Christ Jesus. And if you are Christ's, then you are Abraham's seed, and heirs according to the promise."*

Jesus created a spiritual bottleneck that puts everyone on the same level. Each person will have to pass through the same gate, and accept Him. **John 14:6** *"Jesus said to him, 'I am the way, the truth, and the life. No one comes to the Father except through Me.'"*

In Barbados, there is a gated community named Port St. Charles. It was built by one of our wealthiest citizens, Sir Charles Williams. To build this community, Sir Charles had to create a marina for owners of condos to dock their yachts in front of their respective residences. He did this by removing part of the land itself. He changed the shape of what our country looked like before. Can you imagine what it would have been like to be in the room when he announced his vision for this community? Many of us will never be privy to meetings that will reach national proportions. But when I think of the account of the last supper and the fact that Jesus sat with a doctor, tax collector, and fishermen, I realize how great of a gift Jesus extended to these men and how we are all given a seat at His table.

Reflection & Charge

Do you think you are on the same level as other Christians, or do you see yourself beneath them? **Yes/No**. If no, why do you see yourself as not enough?

Spend some time meditating on the seat that Christ has created for you, at His table. Remember, you are just as valuable as any other person on this planet. Christ has made you an heir of God and co-heir with Himself.

DISARMING THE ENEMY

<u>Movie: 8 Mile (2002)</u>

One of the aliases of the devil is "accuser of the brethren". He takes it upon himself to point out our faults to God to condemn us to live outside of the reality of the grace that comes through Christ. I think we have become great at covering our flaws. When we attend services, we make sure we are wearing our Sunday best; we put on that smile where no one really knows that we are hurting inside. I think we all have had that nightmare of appearing in public naked, totally exposed to the world. Many problems have been kept bottled up, and they have grown and been passed down to the next generation. Sin, like some bacteria, thrives in secret. It operates effectively when it is ignored and festers in the darkest regions of our hearts.

In the rap battle, Jimmy Smith takes the mic first. Knowing that the other MC is going to use some events in his life against him, he reveals all of his weaknesses and flaws before his opponent and the entire crowd. He says he is a bum; he is white; he lives in a trailer with his mother; he was beat up by the same guy and his crew, he even discloses that his girlfriend cheated on him. That stripped his opponent of any ammunition. It disarmed him, so he had nothing to use against Jimmy.

James 5:16 *"Confess your trespasses to one another, and pray for one another, that you may be healed. The effective, fervent prayer of a righteous man avails much."* As believers, we are tasked with taking the Gospel to all nations. There is a generation of people, millennials, and those who come after who do not buy what we are selling. They are calling us out on our lack of transparency and hypocrisy. They see right through us and know that we are not telling the whole truth and nothing but the truth. So, Satan can expose those long held sins we have refused to let go, and uses them to cripple, and make us ineffective to our calling to reach the world.

Revelation 12:10-11 *"Then I heard a loud voice saying in heaven, 'Now salvation, and strength, and the kingdom of our God, and the power of His Christ have come, for the accuser of our brethren, who accused them before our God day and night, has been cast down. And they overcame him by the blood of the Lamb and by the word of their testimony, and they did not love their lives to the death."*

When Jesus Christ died on the cross, He paid for our sins; therefore, Satan has no real claim or power over us apart from sin. Jesus disarmed the Devil, leaving him powerless because he doesn't have the final say in our lives. However, Satan counts on our tendency to operate based on what we have done instead of what Christ has done.

The second part says, *"and by the word of their testimony."* A confession, a willingness to admit our sins and flaws before God, knowing that we are forgiven through the blood of Jesus. The Devil is disarmed, leaving him with no real ammo to keep us living under his authority.

1 John 1:9 *"If we confess our sins, He is faithful and just to forgive us our sins and to cleanse us from all unrighteousness."* I don't believe that God expects us to confess every single sin that we commit. Doing that means we will spend more time trying to identify what we have done wrong instead of focusing on the grace of God. However, when we sin and we are aware, we should confess and not allow the guilt of that sin to weigh on us for too long that Satan can use it against us.

Reflection & Charge

If there are any sins that are lingering in your mind, confess them to God, get it all out, allow Him to know the guilt you feel. Take full responsibility for your choices and embrace the full redemption that is in Christ.

REBIRTH

Movie: The Matrix (1999)

Any person who repents of their sins and confesses Jesus Christ as Lord will experience a new beginning: a rebirth, a new reality. As Christians, we know that the world in which we live is not the only reality. We were born in the physical realm, dominated by our senses and emotions. However, through Christ we have an awareness of the spiritual realm.

> **John 3:5-6** *"Jesus answered, 'Verily, verily, I say unto thee, Except a man be born of water and of the Spirit, he cannot enter into the kingdom of God. That which is born of the flesh is flesh; and that which is born of the Spirit is spirit.'"*

After Neo chooses the red pill, Morpheus and his rebel followers are able to locate his body in the real world and unplug him. Neo comes to realize that he has lived his entire existence in a computer-generated reality built by artificial intelligent robots called the Matrix. The Matrix is a prison created to keep human beings in a state where their actual bodies can be used by the machines as fuel. Neo discovers that as a human being he had an awareness and the ability to operate in the two realities to varying degrees.

Our existence as believers in Christ allows us to be aware of the spiritual realm, and actively take part in it. There are two concepts we must grasp. Although invisible, the spiritual realm is just as real as the physical one; in fact, it might be even more real since our physical bodies and environments will eventually deteriorate. The other concept is that spiritual reality influences the things in the physical one. What we see with our eyes is created from what we don't see.

Hebrews 11:6 *"But without faith it is impossible to please Him, for he who comes to God must believe that He is, and that He is a rewarder of those who diligently seek Him."*

In the book of Luke, a woman among the people Jesus was teaching spent 18 years bent over. The passage describes her condition as spiritual. **Luke 13:11** *"And behold, there was a woman who had a spirit of infirmity eighteen years, and was bent over and could in no way raise herself up."* Jesus speaks to the woman and releases her from the spiritual infirmity that manifested itself physically. This is one of many examples of the spiritual affecting the physical, and it is further confirmation of the two realities we are exposed to when we are unplugged from the sinful nature through Christ.

This means that we should have a heightened awareness of this part of our world. Our attention to this part of ourselves should be increased, realizing that the spirit man will last forever. Sow to the spirit, lay up your treasures in Heaven. Make the activities of the spiritual realm a priority.

"We are not human beings having a spiritual experience; we are spiritual beings having a human experience." - Pierre Teilhard de Chardin.

You don't have to be a believer in Christ to admit that every person has invisible qualities about them. Otherwise, every model or actress would be moral, kind, and care about the needs of others. We are more than our bodies, yet we seem heavily invested in making sure that the outward appearance including our gifts and talents are at their best, while neglecting the inner attributes that God values most.

Reflection & Charge

Make a list of how you spend your week, then categorize that list into spiritual activities and physical activities. Evaluate the amount of energy you spend on each activity and then determine if there needs to be a change in how you spend your time and resources.

Search for scriptures that will help you understand the importance of working on your inner man. Take a look at these three examples: **1 Samuel 16:7; Matthew 23:27-28; 2 Corinthians 4:16.**

MY NAME IS

Mini Series: Roots (1977)

Roots tells the story of Kunta Kinte, an African boy who was kidnapped and brought to America and sold into slavery. During his initial years on the plantation, he tried multiple times to escape his oppressors to return to his home in Africa. After being recaptured from one of his failed attempts to escape, he is strung up in the middle of the plantation and all the slaves and inhabitants of this plantation are forced to watch as he is punished. This was done to discourage the thought of anyone else following Kunta's example.

The slave owner beats Kunta with a whip. Every time he stopped, he would tell the rebellious African to say that his name was Toby, but each time he would respond with a proclamation, *"My name is Kunta Kinte."* The beating continued, and his body became weaker and weaker. With the encouragement of the other slaves, Kunta Kinte finally gives in and announces that his name is Toby. However, Kunta never forgets his name and legacy. It is passed down from himself to his children, and to his children's children for generations.

Shakespeare wrote, *"What is in a name? A rose by any other name would smell just as sweet."* The value of a name does not seem to hold the same significance to us now in 21st century as it did in the past. We choose names because they are popular or after someone we admire. I can use myself as an example, I was named after Carlitos Colon, a retired professional wrestler. We also choose names because they sound cool, or they have a meaning we really want our children to connect with.

In the past, your name connected you to your lineage. In the book of Daniel, the Babylonians are the dominant people in the world and they have successfully conquered many kingdoms, including the Israelites. Daniel was among a group of young men that were elected to serve under the king. Along with changing their diet and their literature, the king changes their name. This is an attempt to erase their connection to their Hebrew roots so they would embrace the Babylonian culture.

Daniel 1:6-7 *"Now from among those of the sons of Judah were Daniel, Hananiah, Mishael, and Azariah. To them the chief of the eunuchs gave names: he gave Daniel the name Belteshazzar; to Hananiah, Shadrach; to Mishael, Meshach; and to Azariah, Abed-Nego."*

What is in a name? Would it matter to you if you discovered that you came from a long line of royalty? Would it matter if your ancestors were a great line of artists or scientists? What if you discovered your name connected you to wealthy landowners or even slave owners? Would it affect the way you see yourself?

As a believer, we have been given a name. **Revelation 2:17** *"He who has an ear, let him hear what the Spirit says to the churches. To him who overcomes I will give some of the hidden manna to eat. And I will give him a* *white stone, and on the stone a new name written which no one knows except him who receives it."*

Society is constantly trying to take this name from us. This world wants to beat us until we forget our spiritual lineage. It is difficult at times to stand on the principles of the word of God in this generation. As soon as you show some objection to a viewpoint or lifestyle, they try to label and cancel you as racist, sexist, sell out, transphobic, or homophobic. The idea now being championed is to have a godless constitution in the new republic. Our Christian worldview is being challenged and attacked every day.

As a citizen of Barbados and an Afro-Caribbean male, the story of Kunta Kinte resonates with me because my ancestors were slaves. In fact, the neighborhood I grew up in and still live was once a plantation powered by the strength of African slaves. I drive by the plantation house daily, which is now owned by a wealthy family on the island.

Like Kunta Kinte, my goal is to pass on to my sons and the next generation the reality of who we were before we were slaves, so they have a sense of their identity. However, as a Christian I am aware of who I am and the spiritual lineage I have in Christ. My natural lineage might include African kings, queens, or other noble people of which I am proud, but my spiritual lineage puts me in the company of the King of Kings. I am surrounded by a great cloud of witnesses, those of the line of David, prophets, kings and priests, and I will not allow the enemy to make me forget my name.

Reflection & Charge

Read Romans 8:17 and Galatians 3:29. They both confirm the spiritual lineage we inherit as believers in Christ. Spend some time meditating and memorizing these passages and allow the word to sink in.

Find someone you can share these verses with or post them on your social media.

A FELL VOICE

Movie: The Lord of the Rings: The Fellowship of the Ring (2001)

Legolas: *"There is a fell voice on the air."*

In the movie LOTR, nine companions set out on a mission to destroy a magical ring by returning to the place of its creation because it is the only way to destroy it. They had to reach their destination, if not, the dark Lord Sauron would recover the ring and become powerful and unstoppable. In one scene, the Fellowship of the Ring chooses a path through the Misty Mountains when they encounter a blizzard. The winds were so strong that they had to abandon this route and instead go under the mountains. Before they decide to turn around, Legolas (an elf) says, *"there is a fell voice on the air."* The word fell in this context means fierce, cruel, malevolent, sinister, or destructive. The voice he is referring to is that of Saruman, a wizard who is speaking a spell in order to conjure the fierce winds against the group.

Matthew 14:30 *"But when he saw that the wind was boisterous, he was afraid; and beginning to sink he cried out, saying, 'Lord, save me!'"*

Jesus demonstrates His deity by defying the laws of nature and walking on water. In this account, Jesus asks Peter to join Him on the water instead of sitting with trepidation. He ignores all the ramifications of a human being able to walk on water and joins Jesus in this supernatural event. Instead of being a spectator, he chooses to be a participant.

To take part in this feat, Peter had to first leave where it was safe, and abandon what seemed reasonable and secure, to go where things appeared uncertain. I guess at that moment he understood the safest place was to be wherever Jesus abides. While he was on the water, he notices the violent wind which was pushing the waves back and forth. It is here I believe he heard a fell voice. The voice however, was an outwardly sinister voice. It was a cruel and destructive voice that reminded Peter that he didn't belong there. It was the voice of the violent wind.

As we launch into new missions and arenas, we will sometimes encounter that fell voice that reminds us we don't belong there. Maybe because of our background, qualifications, or talents. But it is important to note these things are irrelevant to God. We have two options in moments like these: listen to the fell voice, or accept who God says we are and what He has called us to do. If we can ignore the voice, we will move on and walk in purpose.

In the past I would have said the only choice for success was to ignore the voice completely, but we can use the voice as motivation to fight on despite the tactics of the enemy. Don't accept the truths of the voice and sink; call for help from the Lord of the wind and waves. When you recognize your inability to sustain yourself, you will turn to the One who can sustain you, Jesus Christ.

I heard that the most harsh and critical voice in our life is the one that comes from within. Even now, as I am writing, there is a voice that whispers, *"This is a waste of time. People won't want to read what you have written; your ideas are immature."* But I refuse to let that stop me, I will keep on writing. The voice is trying to deter you from moving forward, by telling you that your worst nightmares will come to pass. What if that voice is wrong? Think about all the people who will miss out on whatever God has placed inside of you if you listen to that voice. The only voice you need to follow is that of the Holy Spirit who will guide you into all truth.

Reflection & Charge

Do you find your thoughts are mostly negative? **Yes/No.** If yes, what steps will you take to change this?

What are some of those negative thoughts? List them and replace them with positive ones. See the example below.

Negative thought: "You are not enough."

Positive thought: "God says I am enough."

List Your Negative thoughts here:

List your Positive thoughts here:

ALL MY LIFE I HAD TO FIGHT

Movie: The Color Purple (1985)

"All my life I had to fight." These words were spoken by Sofia in *The Color Purple*. It describes the constant battle she had to face as a woman, by fending off the attacks of men who tried to abuse her. Her character is in anguish as these battles obviously had a tremendous toll on her emotionally, physically, and mentally.

The moment Adam was given a consequence to his disobedience to God, it sparked a chain reaction for the rest of humanity. **Genesis 3:17** *"Then to Adam He said, 'Because you have heeded the voice of your wife, and have eaten from the tree of which I commanded you, saying, You shall not eat of it: Cursed is the ground for your sake; in toil you shall eat of it all the days of your life.'"*

After the fall, Adam had to struggle to provide for himself and his family. Now for us, life is a series of battles as we strive daily to live. Our daily experience is made up of planning and executing tasks to get us from one point to the next. Some of us are fighting to survive, to keep the lights on, to pay the rent / mortgage, to keep our relationships intact with our spouses or children. Some of us are fighting to get to the top, to be recognized and appreciated for our talents, to become successful enough to retire early. Some of us are fighting for our health because our bodies are betraying us to time and sickness. Some are fighting inner battles of past failures and future expectations. Some battles are thrust upon us and others we have created ourselves.

As I get older, I become increasingly aware of my limitations and my inability to defend my circle from the many threats and attacks that life throws at them. I like to hold on to a phrase; *"choose your battles wisely because you don't have the energy to fight them all."*

With the reality of the struggle of life, we look for leadership from our leaders and government officials. In a lot of cases, we are looking to those in these positions to rescue us. This is brought to light when there is some national or global crisis. I have never been interested in politics. When I think of politics, the little play on words comes to mind, politricks, or poly meaning **many tricks**, a blood-sucking insect. You get the idea.

However, I have paid more attention in recent times to hear the ideas that are presented to help the people of our country. I have also been interested because I recognize that as a Christian; I am part of a political system. When I put my faith in Christ, I became a citizen of heaven and with that I have a new political system to which I look to for leadership and guidance.

In Isaiah 9:1-7, there is a popular passage that is usually applied to the prophecy of the birth of Christ. It paints a picture of an oppressed people who now have their hope renewed by the birth of their long-awaited Savior and King. One of the promises made to the people is found in verse 5, *"For every warrior's sandal from the noisy battle, and garments rolled in blood, will be used for burning and fuel of fire."*

There will no longer be a need to fight so hard, all remnants and resources of war will be destroyed and those under the Government of God's Kingdom will no longer have to battle. This is good news because all champions get tired at some point. Trying to hold everything together is exhausting, both to the body and to the mind. Jesus offers rest, first in this life where we can let go of the need to fight the barrage of battles we encounter. Then in our next life where we will live in perfect peace with no need to strive to survive.

Matthew 11:28-30 *"Come to Me, all you who labor and are heavy laden, and I will give you rest. Take My yoke upon you and learn from Me, for I am gentle and lowly in heart, and you will find rest for your souls. For My yoke is easy and My burden is light."*

I don't have enough time or energy to fight every battle. So, there are some battles that are not worth fighting. I won't win all, anyway. Like trying to change people is the one that we all can relate to. The other battles I will allow God to take the lead and fight on my behalf. We are co-laborers with God. There is a role we play, and there is a role only God can handle.

Reflection & Charge

Examine your life and the battles you are currently dealing with. Categorize them into ones that require your specific attention and ones you need to let go.

The things you need to work on:

The things you need to let go:

PLAY OUR GAME

Movie: Coach Carter (2005)

Coach Carter coaches a group of boys and helps them become a basketball team. In the process of their training, he hopes to develop them into more than boys who can win the game of basketball. His intention is to make them men that win at the game of life. In one scene, the Richmond Oilers are behind and struggling against their opponent. Coach Carter calls a timeout and gives them a pep talk. *"All season long we played our game, right now you are playing theirs. When we step on the floor every second that clock is ticking, we are pedal to the metal, we run the ball, we pressure the ball, and most importantly we control the tempo of the game, we make them play Richmond Oiler ball."*

As believers in Christ, we must know the landscape on which we do battle. We have to be aware of the terrain and the rules of engagement. There is an enemy, he is not flesh and blood, but he is spirit. His tactics and strategies are spiritual. In his attempt to derail our walk with Christ, he employs methods where he is sure to win. He plays the game of misdirection, forcing us to use the tactics that are fruitless. He is constantly luring us into playing his game instead of playing ours.

2 Corinthians 10:3-6 *"For though we walk in the flesh, we do not war according to the flesh. For the weapons of our warfare are not carnal but mighty in God for pulling down strongholds, casting down arguments and every high thing that exalts itself against the knowledge of God, bringing every thought into captivity to the obedience of Christ, and being ready to punish all disobedience when your obedience is fulfilled."*

It is imperative that you remember we do not fight like other people do. Our weapons are mighty ones, but they are spiritual ones. It is not a battle of wills or battle of intellect, nor is it a battle of physical force. I watch with great frustration sometimes how some Christians try to win unbelievers to our side by attacking and criticizing them. In Barbados, there is a popular call-in program and each day there is a different moderator who hosts and facilitates the conversations. One of these moderators is a gay atheist who draws some attention especially from the Christian community.

They call in and quote Bible verses, give bile analysis, condemn him to hell, and threaten to boycott the program. The mistake they make is to engage him on the level of intellect, an arena in which he is a formidable opponent. It never ends well, and it always seems to put Christians in an awkward and ineffective position. We are most powerful when we use weapons and resources that are mighty in God.

We may stage walks and protests against abortion or other legislation we see as contrary to our Christian beliefs. What if we are successful in getting them to change a law that supports our belief? What then, will the law change the hearts of men and women? Think of the battles within your homes and workplace, evaluate each one, and see if you gained any ground. If not, that is simply because you are playing their game. You are allowing the enemy to set the rules and pace of the competition.

In the Garden of Gethsemane, after Jesus had finished praying, a group of religious leaders and soldiers come to arrest Him. In his usual brash fashion, Peter draws his sword and attacks Malchus, cutting his ear from his face. Jesus says to Peter, *"Put your sword in its place, for all who take the sword will perish by the sword."* **Matthew 26:52**

Jesus refused to fight the battle in the power of physical or earthly force, instead He surrenders to the will of God and triumphs through the Spirit.

I am not saying we should never debate or defend our faith or stand up for the things we read in the word to be true and right. Of course, we should, but we must consider the timing, forum, and the people we use to spread the message God has given us. Spend more time highlighting why we should follow Christ instead of all the reasons those who don't are wrong.

Reflection & Charge

Take inventory of your spiritual weapons and tactics. This might take some research in the word which by the way is one of your spiritual weapons. Once you have identified your weapons and tactics, apply them to the situations in your life.

DAY 21

DISCIPLINE

Movie: The Last Samurai (2003)

"From the moment they wake, they devote themselves to the perfection of whatever they pursue. I have never seen such discipline." -Captain Algren

In The Last Samurai, Captain Algren (of the Confederate army) has been hired to train Japanese soldiers to fight against a rebel group of samurai warriors, headed by their leader, Katsumoto. After a battle in the woods between the Japanese soldiers and the samurai, Captain Algren was captured by Katsumoto. In his time as prisoner, he observed the lives of the Samurai and was impressed with their commitment and discipline to learning their chosen skill, one of which is mastery of the sword.

One of the symbols used to represent the word of God is a sword. In Ephesians 6:17, Paul defines it as the sword of the Spirit. God has designed this powerful weapon over the centuries through inspiration of a myriad of authors, all with a theme that points to who He is. As believers, it is our responsibility to become intimate with the truths and principles of the Bible. We must dedicate ourselves to learning and applying God's word to our lives. We must become sword masters. **Psalm 1:2** *"But his delight is in the law of the Lord, and in His law he meditates day and night."*

We see an example of the sword being used when the devil tempts Jesus. Every time Satan presents Him with his plan, Jesus responds with a quote from what had already been written by God through the prophets. Each time He begins His defense with, "it is written," a lesson that shows we must know the word in order to be effective.

The devotion of the samurai to their sword is one that leaves me in awe. It is said that they saw the sword as an extension of themselves. If two samurais passed each other and their swords accidentally touched, it would start a conflict between the two. The word of God needs to become part of us. It cannot be something we fit into our schedule; our schedule needs to be built around it. What we read daily must dictate the way we see and perceive the world. It must be the standard to which we work and interact with people, it must be the reference to which we use to make decisions.

When I first had the opportunity to be a leader in church, I encountered some fear and doubt. I was worried that as a preacher, I would run out of things to teach. One story that empowered me to take the step forward was that of the feeding of the 5,000. Jesus took what was inadequate for the situation and made it more than enough. I still felt uncertain about whether I could handle the task and weight of leadership, especially leadership in the Church. The words spoken to Joshua by God in Joshua 1:9 convinced me I could step into the role and the roles that would follow with confidence that God would be with me. *"Have I not commanded you? Be strong and of good courage; do not be afraid, nor be dismayed, for the Lord your God is with you wherever you go."*

I do not consider myself a master of the word, but it is my intention to devote myself to make it as much a part of my life as possible. Our lives are filled with a lot, and it's challenging to find time to read the Bible let alone meditate on it, but its importance cannot be denied. It is essential for our walk with God. Navigating this life without our sword of the Spirit is impossible.

Reflection & Charge

I'm supposed to tell you to look at your busy schedule and find space for reading and studying the word. That approach is ok, but I suggest reorganizing your schedule so that time in the word becomes a priority and other parts fit around it.

Write a schedule below and organize your week by making God's word priority.

SLAVES TO PURPOSE

Movie: The Matrix Reloaded (2003)

"We're not here because we're free; we're here because we're not free. There's no escaping reason, no denying purpose, for as we both know, without purpose we would not exist. It is purpose that created us, purpose that connects us, purpose that pulls us, that guides us, that drives us; it is purpose that defines us, purpose that binds us. We are here because of you, Mr. Anderson. We're here to take from you what you tried to take from us. Purpose." -Agent Smith

When we talk about purpose, we are asking for the reason of something or someone; we basically want to know 'why'. One of the most overused and maybe even abused statement is, "everything happens for a reason." Is that really the case? Does everything happen for a reason? Does everything really have a purpose?

I link purpose to identity, because knowing who you are determines what you are here to do. Or is it the other way around where your purpose defines identity? Like with the chicken or the egg? In the book of John, Jesus and His disciples encounter a man who had been blind from birth. The disciples are of the belief that the blindness is a result of sin. Someone sinned, either it was the man himself or his parents. Jesus corrects this misconception by telling them that the man's blindness exists so that God's work might be displayed.

John 9:1-3 *"Now as Jesus passed by, He saw a man who was blind from birth. And His disciples asked Him, saying, 'Rabbi, who sinned, this man or his parents, that he was born blind?' Jesus answered, 'Neither this man nor his parents sinned, but that the works of God should be revealed in him.'"*

This passage is saying that even the blindness had a purpose. That leads me to wonder about the other ailments, disfunctions, or shortcomings that we struggle with. Do they all have a purpose? Well, I believe everything has purpose, everything has a reason for being, everything has a why. If blindness can have a purpose, then we who are made in the image of God must also have purpose.

John the Baptist was a unique individual. He spent his time in the desert, wore camel's hair as clothing, and his diet comprised of locusts and honey. Regardless of his eccentric character, he was called the greatest of the prophets by Jesus. One of the most intriguing things about John is that he knew why he was on this planet, and he knew it from birth. (Luke 2:15-17, 76-79)

Is it better to know why you exist from the beginning of your life, or is it better to search and discover it along the way? Is it more of a blessing, or is it a burden? Is it a weight or cross you must carry until the task is complete? Are we like Agent Smith suggests, slaves to purpose? Well, a strong sense of purpose allowed John the Baptist to remain on track. He neglected involvement in normal activities and only ate and wore what was essential.

I once attended an art exhibition with my wife, and there were beautiful displays of the talent and creativity that exist among the people in Barbados. One particular section drew my attention, the art was amazing. There were colorful paintings and immaculate sculptures, very detailed and unique. There was a tag which gave the name and address of the artist on all the work. The strange thing about the artists in this section was that the same three letters were written in the line next to the address: HMP, Her Majesty's Prison. I wondered if these individuals had a stronger sense of purpose would it have led them in a different path, one where they would have used their gifts before they ran into trouble. Maybe being in prison happened for a reason and unearthed their purpose.

Now let us get to the part you have been waiting for, the part where I tell you about your purpose, your why. Of course, I don't know you or your talents or abilities, nor do I know your dreams and interests. Despite all of that, I know your purpose. As Christians, we all share the same purpose. **Colossians 1:16** *"For by Him all things were created that are in heaven and that are on earth, visible and invisible, whether thrones or dominions or principalities or powers. All things were created through Him and for Him.*

Just like the blindness, just like John the Baptist, we are all created for Jesus Christ. Our purpose is to point people to God, the One who gave us origin and existence. We may all express this in different ways, but it must be this one thing. **Matthew 5:16** *"Let your light so shine before men, that they may see your good works and glorify your Father in heaven."*

A Rube Goldberg machine, named after American cartoonist Rube Goldberg, is a machine intentionally designed to perform a simple task in an indirect and overly complicated way. The thing about the machine is that although it is complicated, all of its components are intentional and have been well thought out. Your life can sometimes feel complicated and confusing, but everything that happened was allowed to bring about a desired result. Your relationships, experiences, wins, losses, the lessons you have learned and the lessons you have taught are all part of God's Rube Goldberg machine for your life and His purpose. Start being intentional about your life journey, evaluate your decisions, and ask yourself if they are allowing the world to praise God in Heaven.

Reflection & Charge

How does it make you feel to know that your life is a part of this larger picture to point people toward God?

You know your collective purpose in the Body of Christ, but what is your individual purpose?

How are your actions, attitudes, and words giving those around you glimpses of God?

DAY 23

RIDE TOGETHER

Movie: Bad Boys 2 (2003)

I think we all need a ride or die in our life. A person who sticks with us no matter the situation; a person who will tell us we are wrong, but still has our back in a fight. That person who knows our deepest darkest failings and would still take a bullet for us.

In the Bad Boys movie franchise, detectives Marcus Burnett and Michael Lowrey are partners in the Miami Police force. There is one scene where Marcus has to come to grips with the fact that his sister has been kidnapped by a Colombian drug lord and they don't have legal jurisdiction in Mexico to arrest this criminal. Mike reassures him they will have to do it by themselves. *"We ride together, we die together, bad boys for life."*

As Christians, we have a ride or die in Christ. The Bible calls Jesus, Immanuel, God with us. He is God. Whatever essence, substance… the Spirit that makes up God the Father, also dwelled in Jesus Christ. Every time Jesus forgives sinners, we see God. We see God when He heals leprosy, lameness, blindness, or casts out a spirit. We see

God when He walks on water or calms the wind and waves. Then we see Him as man. While we need God's awesome presence in our lives, we also needed Him as man. He is God and with that comes Holiness, this untouchable attribute that creates distance between Himself and us; just ask Uzzah who reached out to steady the cart that was carrying the Ark of the Covenant which represented the Presence of God.

As God, He fed the five thousand people with five loaves and two fish; as man, after 40 days in the wilderness He was hungry. As God He turned water into wine; as man, right before He died, He thirsted. As God, He healed the woman with the issue of blood; as man, when His side was pierced, He bled and died. As God, He is El Shaddai, the all-Sufficient One; as man, He cried, "My God, My God why have You forsaken me?" It is as man that we received an amazing gift, the gift of empathy. He not only feels for us, He also feels with us. This is one of the most significant areas of Christianity, one that separates our beliefs from many others. The Creator walked and lived among His creation, enduring the same struggles and challenges we face. **Hebrews 4:15** *"For we do not have a High Priest who cannot sympathize with our weaknesses, but was in all points tempted as we are, yet without sin."*

Jesus experienced loneliness so He could walk with us through ours. We receive a partner in pain, He shares in ours, and we share in His. We need the God who can light our way out of darkness, but we also need the man who walks with us in the darkness until we reach the light. I don't think we realize that throughout our daily activities we have God's presence with us. Maybe because we think He is there with us only in moments of great emotion and fanfare. However, the Bible proves otherwise.

Jesus was born in a manger, He worked as a carpenter and He rode on a donkey, all lowly activities. After His resurrection, Jesus walked with two disciples but He didn't allow them to recognize Him. He conversed with them for their entire journey and it wasn't until He sat with them and broke bread that they realized it was Him. (Luke 24:13-31). I believe Jesus is with us at every moment. He already died for us, what makes us think that He wouldn't also ride with us.

Reflection & Charge

Have you ever felt as if God was not riding with you? If yes, what was the situation(s)?

THE STRENGTH OF THE PHALANX

Movie: 300 (2006)

King Leonidas: *"Your father should have taught you how our phalanx works. We fight as a single, impenetrable unit. That is the source of our strength. Each Spartan protects the man to his left from thigh to neck with his shield."* [Leonidas takes his sword and shield to demonstrate.]

King Leonidas: *"A single weak spot and the phalanx shatters. From thigh to neck, Ephialtes."*

In the book of Genesis, after Cain had just killed his brother (Abel), God asks Cain, *"Where is Abel?"* Cain responds with a lie, *"I don't know",* and then follows the lie with a question of his own. The question is not one Cain expects an answer, but in this context, he uses it to absolve himself of the responsibility of his brother's wellbeing. However, it is a question which if answered in the affirmative, changes everything.

If we answer yes to this question, then we eradicate poverty. The murder and crime rate may decline if we answer yes to the question. If we answer yes, then our society becomes a safe place for children to grow. If we answer yes, then we no longer live in an era that says every man for himself. If we say yes, we truly acknowledge that we are all in this thing together. What is the question? *"Am I my brother's keeper?"*

The Greek Phalanx was based on the principle of doing your best to protect the man next to you. And with that, you depended on the man to your right to protect you. It created a unified battle formation that was a very successful and almost impenetrable fighting strategy in the days of King Leonidas and his 300 Spartans.

In the book of Acts, we read of a group of people who seemed to have answered this question with an emphatic yes, and created a community with true unity.

Acts 4:32-35 *"Now the multitude of those who believed were of one heart and one soul; neither did anyone say that any of the things he possessed was his own, but they had all things in common. And with great power the apostles gave witness to the resurrection of the Lord Jesus. And great grace was upon them all. Nor was there anyone among them who lacked; for all who were possessors of lands or houses sold them, and brought the proceeds of the things that were sold, and laid them at the apostles' feet; and they distributed to each as anyone had need."*

This situation almost seems too good to be true, a group of people were willing to ensure that there was no lack among them. No apparent selfishness or selfish ambition, but a genuine concern and attentiveness to the welfare of each other. For a community like this to exist, it meant there had to be a lack of judgment of a person's situation. There also had to be a sense of safety and security that made it possible for a person to share or acknowledge their lack.

This group of people came to realize the Holy Spirit was the giver of everything they had. We take pride in the things we have earned, but truly it is the Lord who gives us strength to get wealth. Even when that wealth is mental, emotional, or even spiritual, we should make sure we share with others.

What would it be like to be part of a community where you felt safe to open up? One where you can acknowledge your shortcomings, knowing that you won't be judged or discarded. I think we would all love to be a part of this community. A safe zone, one where the real you could be exposed and you could find healing. **James 5:16** *"Confess your trespasses to one another, and pray for one another, that you may be healed. The effective, fervent prayer of a righteous man avails much."*

Are we truly our brothers or sisters' keepers? When we ask our neighbors, "how are you doing?" Do we really want to hear the messy truth of their struggling relationships or their inability to pay off debts? Do we really want to hear that they are not making it, or do we prefer them to just cover their pain with a smile and give a brilliant response? The concept of "mind your business" is one that must be reevaluated so that we don't ignore the pain and struggle of those who we call brother or sister. It should be, "your problem is my problem."

Reflection & Charge

Are you your brother's keeper? If yes, explain how.

If something is wrong with your fellow brother/sister in Christ, will you help carry their burden? If yes, explain how.

When you ask people, "how are you", do you really want to know or are you doing it out of courtesy?

Pay attention to the people around you, sometimes people are fighting silent battles and need help and encouragement. Don't be so self-absorbed. How can you work on being a better brother/sister in Christ?

MY BELIEFS DO NOT REQUIRE YOU TO

Movie: The Matrix Reloaded (2003)

In the Matrix Reloaded, everyone is not in agreement with the path that Morpheus is taking. He believes in a prophecy that tells of the one who will return to liberate the remnant of the human race from the bondage of Artificial Intelligence. I admire his resolve and his willingness to act even though others didn't hold to his belief.

I have struggled throughout my life with an addiction, and it has caused some conflict with those who are close to me. I was addicted to approval. My dominant love language is words of affirmation, so I have an issue with people not liking me. I usually try not to enter debates about different beliefs. However, over time I have felt the strong urge to present my beliefs as aggressively as I can, expecting opposition and disapproval.

There is an instance in the Gospels where Jesus is called to a village because His friend Lazarus is dead. By the time He arrives, Lazarus has been dead for four days. The family and friends of the deceased are distraught and emotional, pondering why Jesus didn't come earlier knowing that His presence would have prevented this result. It is here we find the shortest verse in the Bible and a demonstration of emotion from Christ. **John 11:35** *"Jesus wept."* But why?

He obviously had the power to raise Lazarus, so why display emotions as if the situation was hopeless? His weeping showed His connection to Lazarus and His empathy for those who felt the loss. He understood how they felt and their perspective, although His perspective was different. He understood although He didn't agree. I often encounter people who don't see things the way I do, their claim is always that I don't understand. I am always careful to rebut their claims by offering an interpretation of their views giving evidence that I understand…I just don't agree. It is quite possible for us to understand each other without having to agree.

It is liberating to accept the mindset of Morpheus. His beliefs did not need external validation for him to hold true to them. I want everybody to see things as I do, but I also recognize this is highly improbable. I will have to be obedient to what I believe is my calling, whether people understand or agree with me.

To avoid chaos where people are just doing whatever comes to their minds, we must ensure that our calling is from God. Our beliefs must be in alignment with the word of God. Anything we are pursuing or holding to must have clear biblical justification. We will then have the courage and internal fortitude necessary to stand against any naysayers and opposition.

Paul makes an argument where he says that we should not cause another to stumble because we differ in an area of belief. This calls for us to be convinced in our own minds about the path we are to follow and be committed to said path in faith.

Romans 14:5 *"One person esteems one day above another; another esteems every day alike. Let each be fully convinced in his own mind."* I will admit, it feels good when others agree with you, but as time passes, there are fewer people who agree with the Christian principles I hold dear. There are so many denominations and subgroups in Christianity, so there are more points in doctrine to disagree on.

I realize that I sometimes hold back on moving forward with a task because I am waiting for someone to say that I am on the right track. However, I am learning it will be necessary sometimes to stand alone to accomplish God's mission for your life.

Reflection & Charge

Identify any area in your life where you have not moved forward because you are waiting for external validation from others.

Pray for the strength and courage to take the steps necessary to accomplish this task in God's timing.

NO ONE IS FREE UNTIL WE ARE ALL FREE

Series: Underground (2016-2017)

Underground tells the story of a group of slaves who plot and eventually make an escape from their plantation and its master. They are aided by the members of the Underground Railroad. At the end of the first season most of those who ran are dead or have been captured, only two make it to freedom, a young girl and Rosalee (a house slave). However, Rosalee is not content with freedom knowing that they are others who are still enslaved, so she goes back. Rosalee says, *"No one is free until we are all free."*

Joshua 1:10-15 *"Then Joshua commanded the officers of the people, saying, pass through the camp and command the people, saying, 'Prepare provisions for yourselves, for within three days you will cross over this Jordan, to go in to possess the land which the Lord your God is giving you to possess.' And to the Reubenites, the Gadites, and half the tribe of Manasseh Joshua spoke, saying, 'Remember the word which Moses the servant of the Lord commanded you, saying, The Lord your God is giving you rest and is giving you this land.' Your wives, your little ones, and your* *livestock shall remain in the land which Moses gave you on this side of the Jordan. But you shall pass before your brethren armed, all your mighty men of valor, and help them, until the Lord has given your brethren rest, as He gave you, and they also have taken possession of the land which the Lord your God is giving them. Then you shall return to the land of your possession and enjoy it, which Moses the Lord's servant gave you on this side of the Jordan toward the sunrise.*'"

Joshua and the Israelites stand on the threshold of history. They are about to cross into Canaan, the Promised land. All that separates them from all that they have dreamed of for centuries is a river. Before they cross over, he addresses the officers so they can pass the message to the people. He tells them to get ready to take possession, but to a particular group he reminds them of their promise.

These two and half tribes do not need to cross over and engage in battle. They have their land and inheritance. However, they cannot enjoy it until the rest of the Israelites have their land as well. They are instructed to leave their possessions behind and cross the Jordan to fight with the rest of the Israelites until the conflict is over and they are victorious.

I believe our culture conditions us to compete against each other. We set goals for ourselves, and if we are fortunate enough to achieve those goals, we call ourselves successful. Though I think it is good to celebrate our achievements, I don't think success is complete until those around us have also achieved their goals. We must then rewrite our goals to include the success of the other members of our community. **1 Corinthians 12:26** *"And if one member suffers, all the members suffer with it; or if one member is honored, all the members rejoice with it."*

Paul rightfully says, we can be content in all things, but still reach forward to greater things. We can rejoice with those who are rejoicing, but weep with those who are weeping. It is this ability that allows us to celebrate our triumphs and give God thanks for them, but still understand that there is a need for the next person to reach their success as well.

"The strength of the team is each individual team member. The strength of each member is the team." -Phil Jackson

I heard someone use an illustration of a boat where two people are paddling in the direction of their goal. He said we must make sure that we row with people who are paddling in the same direction as us. I agree with the idea that if you are going to accomplish something in life, it is necessary to build the right team. We have to find people who will buy into the dream we believe God has given us to fulfill.

Reflection & Charge

Find someone and ask them how you can contribute to something they are trying to achieve. Two is sometimes better than one, if you need help with something you are working on, don't be afraid to ask for help.

WANT VS. NEED

Movie: Soul (2020)

Matthew 9:1-2 *"So He got into a boat, crossed over, and came to His own city. Then behold, they brought to Him a paralytic lying on a bed. When Jesus saw their faith, He said to the paralytic, 'Son, be of good cheer; your sins are forgiven you.'"*

Your sins are forgiven? Didn't Jesus see that this man came to have his lame condition addressed? Obviously, the friends who brought their paralyzed friend believed that there was one who could cure him. Why not just give them what they all wanted, why not give them what was in His power to give? Many of us journey through life with goals and objectives we have set for ourselves. We have great desires that we pursue passionately, believing that if these desires are met, we will be happy or fulfilled. The man and his friends were looking for healing, but what the man really needed was to have his sins forgiven. Jesus knew it wasn't a physical condition that needed attention, but a spiritual one.

In the animated film *Soul*, the main character wants desperately to achieve the goal of becoming a star musician. Joe says, *"Music is all I think about. From the moment I wake up in the morning to the moment I fall asleep at night."* He believes that his life will not begin until he reaches this goal of playing for a particular singer. His incredible talent and musical ability open a door for him to have this dream realized, but then he dies.

The rest of the movie is centered on Joe doing all he could to escape the afterlife and get back to this chance of a lifetime. He is eventually successful, but realizes that he is still empty. He only realizes at the end that he had been so blind in his pursuit of becoming a famous musician, he didn't recognize all the moments that had already made his life worth living.

Like Joe, the balancing act between our wants and needs can be challenging. It is one that I recently learned in storytelling to help develop a character. We resonate with those characters that struggle with this internal battle. We cheer on our favorite characters and heroes as they pursue some external goal, but we connect when we see them realize and receive the thing they need.

Amid all that we are chasing after, our greatest need is for the Savior, to have the weight of sin lifted from our hearts. It is only after giving the paralyzed man what he needed, did Jesus address what he wanted. In fact, it didn't even seem like Jesus was going to heal this man until he discerned the thoughts of the naysayers around Him.

Paul was well acquainted with the idea of needs and wants, he prayed for a thorn to be taken away from His life, but that request was denied and he had to live the rest of his life without having this desire met. **2 Corinthians 12:8-9** *"Concerning this thing I pleaded with the*

Lord three times that it might depart from me. And He said to me, 'My grace is sufficient for you, for My strength is made perfect in weakness.' Therefore most gladly I will rather boast in my infirmities, that the power of Christ may rest upon me."

It is an important lesson for us because there are things we want that we may never have. We may pray for a miracle, or long for a supernatural intervention that may never materialize, so we need to be intimately aware of our need for Jesus and His grace. **Mark 8:36** *"For what will it profit a man if he gains the whole world, and loses his own soul?"*

There are times when I see a person who is disabled, and I am certain that at some point they wished or prayed to be healed. Why didn't it work? Why didn't God heal them? Why did He allow the circumstance to occur in the first place? Is it because they didn't have enough faith, or was it not the right time? Maybe they will live with that condition for the rest of their life, but somewhere in there may be an opportunity for them to trust God beyond what He can do for them and learn to love Him for who He is.

Reflection & Charge

If you are not getting the things that you have been praying to God for, maybe there is a greater need that God is working on fulfilling in your life. Reevaluate the things that you have been asking God to give you, the things you have dreamed about having. Pray instead that God would show you the things that will display His truth and grace in you. Write your prayer below.

GIVE THEM WHAT THEY DESERVE

Movie: Lord of the Rings: The Return of the King (2003)

Gollum is one of the major characters in the Lord of the Rings. Whether he is a villain or a victim is hard to decide. He is a sickly looking and vile creature who is motivated by one thing, to be reunited with his precious: the ring. He will lie, steal, and even kill if necessary to get the ring back in his possession. He stalks our heroes as they try to complete the mission to destroy this magical ring. Gandalf responds to Frodo who bemoans the fact that Bilbo (his uncle) and a character from the prequel, The Hobbit, should have killed Gollum.

Frodo: *"It's a pity Bilbo didn't kill Gollum when he had the chance."*

Gandalf: *"Pity? It was pity that stayed Bilbo's hand. Many that live deserve death. Some that die deserve life. Can you give it to them, Frodo? Do not be too eager to deal out death in judgment."*

Jonah 1:7-9 *"And they said to one another, 'Come, let us cast lots, that we may know for whose cause this trouble has come upon us.' So they cast lots, and the lot fell on Jonah. Then they said to him, 'Please tell us! For* *whose cause is this trouble upon us? What is your occupation? And where do you come from? What is your country? And of what people are you?' So he said to them, 'I am a Hebrew; and I fear the Lord, the God of heaven, who made the sea and the dry land.'"*

Jonah is a prophet; and a prophet's job is to hear the message from God and deliver it to the people. But Jonah is not simply a prophet, he is a prophet on the run! He is given a task to go to Nineveh. Obviously, there is something about the task that is unappealing to Jonah because he runs away. What follows is an epic adventure, a real whale of a tale.

The ship he boards is being tossed back and forth in a storm. The crew is terrified, believing that the cause of the storm is not natural, so they cast lots and discover that somehow Jonah is the culprit. They question him, wanting to know who he truly was and why he was the source of this storm. The crew throws Jonah into the sea, which causes the storm to stop. As he descends into the depths of the sea, he is swallowed by a great fish. There is a major debate among scientists and religious leaders on whether this is possible. It is good enough for me that the author writes, "the Lord prepared a fish." After three days of praying from inside this fish, Jonah is vomited onto dry land and carries the message to the people of Nineveh.

If we fast forward to Chapter 4, we find out the reason Jonah decided it wasn't in his best interest to warn the people of Nineveh of the wrath of God. **Jonah 4:1-2** *"But it displeased Jonah exceedingly, and he became angry. So he prayed to the Lord, and said, 'Ah, Lord, was not this what I said when I was still in my country? Therefore I fled previously to Tarshish; for I know that You are a gracious and merciful God, slow to anger and abundant in lovingkindness, One who relents from doing harm.'"*

Jonah never believed that these people deserved to be spared, but as soon as these citizens from Nineveh heard the warning, they turned and asked for God to have mercy on them and God does. Jonah is upset at this; he would have preferred they died by God's hand. How could Jonah decide these people were not worthy of salvation? What gave him the right to decide who lived and who died? It is easy to cast a judgmental eye on Jonah, but with a deeper analysis I realize how alike I am to him. Sometimes when I recall some of the injustices I see in our world, I am angered. In my opinion, there are some people so vile and wicked that an eternity of torment is a few millennia too short for the things they have done.

I am sure you don't have to exercise a lot of mental energy to come up with people who you believe deserve to go without salvation. My mind always goes back to those cruel African traders who sold their African brothers into slavery and the Europeans who bought them and abused them mentally, physically, and spiritually in order to build their empires of wealth. Today, many of the descendants of those same slave owners still reap the benefits of the atrocities of these realities.

Who am I to decide who deserves God's mercy? How can I objectively look at the people in this world and judge them? After all, I am one of the fortunate ones on whom His mercy rests. I wonder if there is someone out there who thinks I didn't deserve it either. **Romans 9:15** *'For He says to Moses, 'I will have mercy on whomever I will have mercy, and I will have compassion on whomever I will have compassion.'"*

Reflection & Charge

Who are the people you believe are not worthy of salvation?

Now that you have written your list, pray for them consistently. There is no one who has gone so far from God that cannot repent.

THE FELLOWSHIP OF THE CROSS

Movie: The Lord of the Rings: The Fellowship of the Ring (2001)

In the first installment of the Lord of the Rings, a group of companions set out on an epic journey with one purpose. They must destroy the ring of power before the dark Lord Sauron gets it and uses it to overthrow all of Middle Earth. The members of the group are diverse, they are from the race of Elves, Dwarves, Wizards, Men, and Hobbits. Because of their willingness to join forces to take the ring to Mordor to the fires of Mount Doom where it was created, they become the Fellowship of the Ring.

Nehemiah 2:17-18 *"Then I said to them, 'You see the distress that we are in, how Jerusalem lies waste, and its gates are burned with fire. Come and let us build the wall of Jerusalem, that we may no longer be a reproach.' And I told them of the hand of my God which had been good upon me, and also of the king's words that he had spoken to me. So they said, 'Let us rise up and build.' Then they set their hands to this good work."*

Nehemiah, a Jewish exile living in Persia sets out on an epic quest. The walls of the once great and powerful Jerusalem are in ruins and because of it, the Jewish people have been living in disgrace and shame. Nehemiah has returned to Jerusalem to gather the people together to take on an important task of rebuilding the walls and restoring the Jews to a place of dignity and strength.

The people who put their hands to the work were from different backgrounds. They were priests, perfumers, goldsmiths, district leaders, and every person or group had a specific project to complete. They worked on different sections of the wall, but they were all working on the same wall. The thing we are part of is bigger than the part we play. I imagine there were people working on the wall who could not see each other, but they worked believing that the other person was working as hard as they were.

Every movement has opposition. This life just by nature introduces opposition. **John 16:33** *"These things I have spoken to you, that in Me you may have peace. In the world you will have tribulation; but be of good cheer, I have overcome the world."*

Newton's Third Law of Motion: For every action, there is an equal and opposite reaction. Every hero has a villain. Nehemiah and the builders of the wall had Sanballat and Tobiah. We all face opposition, sometimes from people who don't want us to succeed and believe our success will put them at a disadvantage. Sometimes it comes from the people who we thought were for us, people who are genuinely afraid that we won't succeed, and others who believe that nobody else should be able to accomplish what they could not. Behind it all is our adversary. He is the major driving force behind opposition to God's work. He employs the help of those around us, or he can play on emotions, fear, jealousy, and selfishness.

Newton's law uses the terms equal and opposite, but while Satan might be opposite to God, he definitely is not equal. Luke 10:18 And He said to them, *"…I saw Satan fall like lightning from heaven."* When he fell, he took one-third of the angels with him. That means two-thirds were left, it means that angels outnumber demons two to one.

In the Lord of the Rings, when the fellowship hear Boromir blow the horn of Gondor, they turn and run to the direction of the sound to fight and defend that position. Nehemiah gives instructions to the people to rally together. If they ever hear the horn blow, it means there is some threat and all must gather to that position to fight. **Nehemiah 4:20** *"Wherever you hear the sound of the trumpet, rally to us there. Our God will fight for us."*

We must work to build the Kingdom, to expand its reach and influence across the globe, to ensure that the truth of this Kingdom is presented accurately and effectively to every living creature. Each person, each church or ministry must recognize that they have a part to play in this project. Our personal lives and ministry may be our responsibility, but they are still a part of the Kingdom.

There is a quote that says *"blood is thicker than water"*, implying that those who share the same DNA should stick closer to each other than any other relationship. As believers in Christ, we might not have the same physical DNA but we have the same spiritual one. The same blood that was shed to cover my sins was shed to cover yours. We are all united by the blood of Jesus Christ. The nine companions in the story might have been dubbed the Fellowship of the Ring. We are the fellowship of the cross.

Reflection & Charge

As part of the fellowship of the cross, each of us has a role to play. Have you identified yours? Spend some time praying about your role, then create a personal mission statement that guides you in how you will play your role effectively.

I SEE YOU

Movie: Avatar (2009)

In Avatar, the aliens greet each other by saying, *"I see you"*. This represents the connection they have with each other. They see more than the physical person; they see the soul and heart of that person. I think the best villains in any story are those who have multiple dimensions. They are not evil for just being evil, but they are heroes in their own stories trying to accomplish some worthy task in their own eyes.

Their perspective makes their cause whether it is detrimental to others, one that is righteous and worthy of pursuit. These characters can sometimes garner sympathy from the audience. I will bet that you cheered John Archibald in *John Q* as he held hostages in a hospital and forced the hospital administration to approve a surgery that would save his son's life. Maybe you are a fan of the *Good Girls* who became bank robbers, money launderers, and gangsters so that they could rescue their families from financial ruin.

In those stories, the characters resonate with us because we can see beyond their obvious illegal and even immoral actions and see their motive. In our minds, we have judged them as worthy. I believe that all of us want to be seen and understood. We want people to recognize the inner motivations that linger beneath the surface of our daily facades. We want people to judge our sometimes unrighteous words and actions as desperate cries for attention.

Genesis 16 tells the story of an Egyptian woman named Hagar, the maidservant of Sarai. In a twisted series of events, Hagar becomes pregnant by Abram, the forefather of the people of Israel and the husband of Sarai. Hagar, seeing that she is able to have children, a feat which her mistress cannot accomplish, becomes indignant to Sarai, and this creates a conflict between the two women. Sarai mistreats her maidservant and so Hagar feels compelled to run away and ends up alone in the wilderness.

It is in this moment of loneliness that the angel of God appears to Hagar and reveals to her that the son she carries will be a great nation. He then instructs her to return to Abram. This event inspires Hagar to call God El Roi, "the God who sees me". It is at this moment of loneliness that God shows up to comfort Hagar. **Genesis 16:13** *"Then she called the name of the Lord who spoke to her, You-Are-the-God-Who-Sees; for she said, 'Have I also here seen Him who sees me?'"*

He is still El Roi; He sees us in the deepest and intimate way. He knows our lives were marred and covered in sin. This is the reason Christ came into the world, to remove the shroud of sin and give us the opportunity to be purified that our lives with align with a purpose that is pure and righteous. Even after we are saved and we struggle, He still sees us, understanding our internal battle to be understood.

Imagine if everyone in this world had one person who could say, "I see you." Imagine if every person had one person in this world who truly could say, "I get you." Imagine if every person in this world knew El Roi.

I remember wishing as a teenager to be popular, to be in a position where everybody knew my name. I got my wish when I pursued tertiary level education. At last, people knew who I was, they knew my name, but although everyone knew me, I still felt alone. The people around me didn't know me. I guess that was really my fault; I didn't show them who I was, and maybe they didn't take the time to dig deeper to find out.

You and I are not just another face in the crowd. There is one person who definitely gets us, there is a God who is well acquainted with our emotions even the ones we can't quite understand or express ourselves.

Reflection & Charge

Write the name given to God by Hagar, El Roi. Every time you see it, read it aloud and remind yourself of its meaning, *"the God who sees me"*. You can take it further by following in the example of the Good Samaritan who stopped and paid attention to the need of another. Try to look deeper than the actions and attitudes of the people who you encounter, make an effort to be the one who sees another for who they really are.

WE ARE STILL HERE

Movie: The Matrix Reloaded (2003)

"Believe me when I say we have a difficult time ahead of us. But if we are to be prepared for it, we must first shed our fear of it. I stand here, before you now, truthfully unafraid." -Morpheus

Morpheus stands before the last human beings on earth in the city of Zion to embolden them as they face an uncertain future. An army of Artificial Intelligence is digging its way through metal and earth somewhere deep in the earth with one aim, destroy every living soul in Zion.

Qué será, será

Whatever will be, will be

The future's not ours to see

Qué será, será

What will be, will be

I remember as a little boy my mother would respond to my questions about the future by singing the lyrics to a song. It was honestly annoying, but it sums up the future. None of us can give a detailed description of what the future holds for ourselves, the world, or even the Church, but what is clear is, as long as we live on this Earth, we will face challenges. There will be failure, sickness, heartbreak, and disappointment. People will leave our lives, betray us, and turn against us. Like the people of Zion, there is an element of uncertainty in our lives.

"No, I stand here without fear because I remember. I remember that I am here not because of the path that lies before me but because of the path that lies behind me. I remember that for 100 years we have fought these machines. I remember that for 100 years they have sent their armies to destroy us, and after a century of war I remember that which matters most… We are still here!" – Morpheus

Morpheus attempts to change their perspective. He is adamant that they can lay aside their fear not because He is certain of what lays ahead, but because of the triumphs of their past. Even though the machines have consistently tried to destroy the human race, they always survived.

Whatever happened before in your life, you are still here. And that is a testament to the grace and purpose of God for your life. We must also examine our collective past as members of the Church. Through persecution, gossip, strife and division, the Church still stands. The scripture says, *"on this rock I will build my church and the gates of hell will not prevail against it."* It may not resemble the early Church described in Acts, but it still stands. Jesus said in this life we would have trouble, but He also said to take heart because He has overcome the world. Jesus has conquered every aspect of life and has empowered us to do the same.

Psalm 1:1-3 *"Blessed is the man who walks not in the counsel of the ungodly, nor stands in the path of sinners, nor sits in the seat of the scornful; but his delight is in the law of the Lord, and in His law he meditates day and night. He shall be like a tree planted by the rivers of water, that brings forth its fruit in its season, whose leaf also shall not wither; and whatever he does shall prosper."*

Psalm 1 paints a picture of the future for believers who will refrain from taking their cues from the ungodly and instead delight in the principles, rules and perspectives of God and meditate on them day and night. They have discovered the inspiring narratives, the practical principles, and the liberating truths of the word of God. The future for them is quite clear. They will be like a tree planted by rivers of water. In other words, they will have access to a source of nourishment which will give them the ability to produce the fruits of righteousness. It isn't a promise of a life free from struggle or pain; it is a promise that we will be able to stand. **Isaiah 26:3** *"You will keep him in perfect peace, whose mind is stayed on You, because he trusts in You."*

"If you are depressed you are living in the past. If you are anxious you are living in the future. If you are at peace you are living in the present." -Lao Tzu

Reflection & Charge

Sometimes we are so preoccupied with what could happen that we forget about the joy of living in the present. What are your greatest fears of your future?

Try to pinpoint where those fears came from.

Remembering what God has done for you before is a great way to stay encouraged when life gets hard. Make a list of the times you thought you were at the end of your rope, but God came through. Write them down and stick them in a place where you could see them every time you enter the room.

REFERENCES

Brackett, Leigh, et al. Star Wars: Episode V - The Empire Strikes Back. Directed by Irvin Kershner, N/A, 1980, N/A.

Cameron, James. Avatar. Directed by James Cameron, N/A, 2009, N/A.

Coogler, Ryan, et al. Black Panther. Directed by Ryan Coogler, N/A, 2018, N/A.

Docter, Pete, et al. Soul. Directed by Pete Docter and Kemp Powers, N/A, 2020, N/A.

Gallo, George, et al. Bad Boys II. Directed by Michael Bay, N/A, 2003, N/A.

Gilroy, Tony, et al. The Bourne Identity. Directed by Doug Liman, N/A, 2002, N/A.

Green, Misha, and Joe Pokaski. Underground. 2016.

Haley, Alex. Roots. Directed by Marvin J. Chomsky, John Erman, David Greene, Gibert Moses, 1977.

Homer, and David Benioff. Troy. Directed by Wolfgang Petersen, N/A, 2004, N/A.

King, Stephen, and Frank Darabont. The Shawshank Redemption. Directed by Frank Darabont, N/A, 1994, N/A.

Logan, John, et al. The Last Samurai. Directed by Edward Zwick, N/A, 2003, N/A.

Meyjes, Menno, and Alice Walker. The Color Purple. Directed by Steven Spielberg, N/A, 1986, N/A.

Nolan, Jonathan, and Christopher Nolan. Interstellar. Directed by Christopher Nolan, N/A, 2014, N/A.

Ross, Gary, et al. The Hunger Games. Directed by Gary Ross, N/A, 2012, N/A.

Schwahn, Mark, and John Gatins. Coach Carter. Directed by Thomas Carter, N/A, 2005, N/A.

Silver, Scott. 8 Mile. Directed by Curtis Hanson, N/A, 2002, N/A.

Snyder, Zack, et al. 300. Directed by Zack Snyder, N/A, 2007, N/A.

Terrio, Chris, et al. Batman v Superman: Dawn of Justice. Directed by Zack Snyder, N/A, 2016, N/A.

The Lord of the Rings: The Return of the King. Directed by Peter Jackson, N/A, 2003, N/A.

The Matrix Reloaded. Directed by Lana Wachowski and Lilly Wachowski, N/A, 2003, N/A.

Tolkien, et al. The Lord of the Rings: The Fellowship of the Ring. Directed by Peter Jackson, N/A, 2001, N/A.

Wachowski, Lilly, and Lana Wachowski. The Matrix. Directed by Lana Wachowski and Lilly Wachowski, N/A, 1999, N/A.

Walsh, Fran, et al. The Hobbit: An Unexpected Journey. Directed by Peter Jackson, N/A, 2012, N/A.

Wenk, Richard, et al. The Equalizer. Directed by Antoine Fuqua, N/A, 2014, N/A.

Woolverton, Linda, et al. Beauty and the Beast. Directed by Gary Trousdale and Kirk Wise, N/A, 1991, N/A.